LIVING *THE* GREAT COMMISSION *IN* MADAGASCAR

LIVING *THE* GREAT COMMISSION *IN* MADAGASCAR

THE STORY OF
MY MISSIONARY FAMILY
FROM THE
DIARY OF
CLARA BRAATEN

CARL E. BRAATEN

ARCHWAY
PUBLISHING

Copyright © 2023 Carl E. Braaten.

All rights reserved. No part of this book may be used or reproduced by any means, graphic, electronic, or mechanical, including photocopying, recording, taping or by any information storage retrieval system without the written permission of the author except in the case of brief quotations embodied in critical articles and reviews.

This book is a work of non-fiction. Unless otherwise noted, the author and the publisher make no explicit guarantees as to the accuracy of the information contained in this book and in some cases, names of people and places have been altered to protect their privacy.

Archway Publishing books may be ordered through booksellers or by contacting:

Archway Publishing
1663 Liberty Drive
Bloomington, IN 47403
www.archwaypublishing.com
844-669-3957

Because of the dynamic nature of the Internet, any web addresses or links contained in this book may have changed since publication and may no longer be valid. The views expressed in this work are solely those of the author and do not necessarily reflect the views of the publisher, and the publisher hereby disclaims any responsibility for them.

ISBN: 978-1-6657-3993-1 (sc)
ISBN: 978-1-6657-3992-4 (e)

Library of Congress Control Number: 2023904072

Print information available on the last page.

Archway Publishing rev. date: 03/09/2023

Dedicated to All the Lutheran Missionaries
Who Planted the Christian Church in Madagascar

CONTENTS

Acknowledgments xiii

Preface xv

Part 1: The Personal Diary of my Mother, Clara Agnes Braaten . . . 1

Postscript by the Editor 91

Photos 98

Part 2: Tales of a Missionary Kid Growing Up in Madagascar. . . .110

Photos 131

About the Book 137

About the Author 139

Mother at her desk with a Malagasy lady

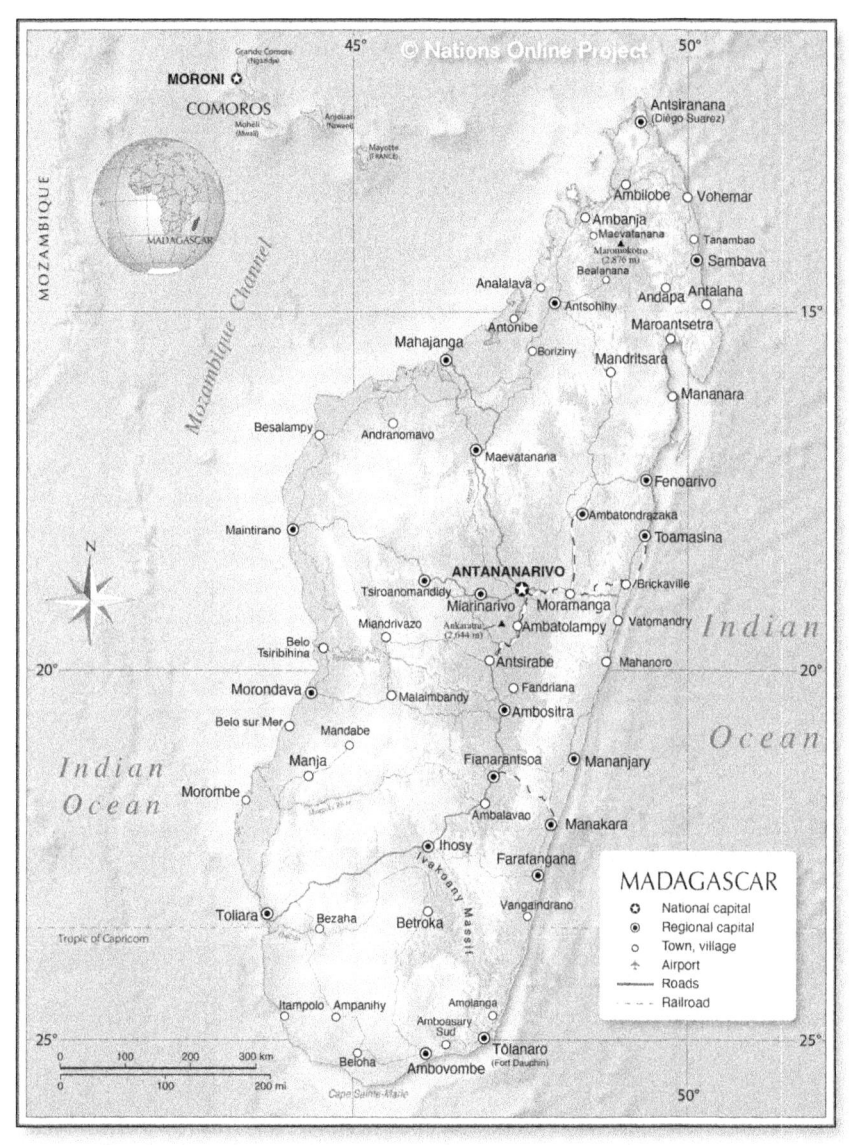

N. B. I am pleased to credit the Nations Online
Project for the use of the above map.

ACKNOWLEDGMENTS

Many hands have contributed to the making of this book. I was encouraged by family members to bring to the light of day the personal diary of my mother, Clara Braaten, the grandmother of my four children, Craig, Martha, Maria, and Kristofer, the great grandmother of Craig's four children, Jennifer, James, Sylvia, and Linnea, Martha's two children, Jake and Dana, Maria's two children, Sean and Sonja, and Kristofer's three children, Ransom, Lennon, and Bergen, and the great grandmother of Jennifer's two children, Jonathan and Carson, James' three children, Rylee, Carly, and Jameson, and Linnea's child, Micah. May the Braaten tribe increase!

I was encouraged along the way by my wife, Beryl, to keep plugging along to the finish line. A huge debt of gratitude I owe to my daughter, Martha Memmesheimer, who was engaged from the start in editing, proof reading, and getting the photos ready for print. We also wish to acknowledge the help of a number of family members who shared albums in their possession with a great variety of photographs from the years my parents served as missionaries in Madagascar — Carolyn Akland, my sister Agnes's daughter, Dianne Moen, my sister Arlene's daughter, Mark Braaten, my brother F. Martin's son, and Jennifer Sayler, Craig's daughter.

PREFACE

My mother, Clara Agnes Braaten, kept a diary from the year she married my father, Torstein Folkvard Braaten, in 1922 until she was ninety four years old, living in California with my sister Agnes and her husband, Dr. Leonard Akland. Three weeks after they were married, they departed Minneapolis by train for New York City to board the Stavangerfjord, a fine Norwegian ocean liner, to cross the Atlantic Ocean on their way to Bergen, Norway, the country of my father's birth. My father had accepted a call from the Foreign Mission Board of the Norwegian Lutheran Church in America to become a missionary to Madagascar. They decided to visit Norway on their way to Paris, France, where they were to spend one year learning the French language. My father had left Norway thirteen years earlier to emigrate to the United States, preceded by two older brothers, Kittel and Olaf. My mother had never been to Norway but her parents had emigrated from Norway decades earlier.

I have entitled this book, *Living the Great Commission in Madagascar*, because the reason my parents decided to become missionaries was to respond, like thousands of others in the nineteenth century, to the Great Commission of our Lord, "Go therefore and make disciples of all nations, baptizing them in the name of the Father and of the Son and of the Holy Spirit." (Matthew 28: 19) That is what they did. They not only obeyed the Great Commission, they lived it every day through thick and thin on the mission field in Madagascar, as my mother recounts in several volumes of her diary. I have read them from time to time, but I was so involved in my own teaching profession, writing books and articles and editing journals of theology, that I kept them on a library shelf until at some later date I might figure out what to do with them. That time has now come. I have decided to edit them in such a way as to tell the story of the life and work of my parents during their thirty five years as missionaries.

Part One of this book consists of excerpts selected from my mother's personal diary. Part Two is a brief narrative of what I remember of my growing up years in Madagascar, until I left for my senior year of high school at Augustana Academy in Canton, South Dakota. This part of the story will include biographical information about my siblings, my two older sisters, Agnes Theodora and Arlene Marie, and my older brother, Folkvard Martin, as well as things I remember of the life we shared at the Missionary Children's Home in Fort Dauphin, a port city at the very southern tip of the island of Madagascar.

PART ONE

The Personal Diary of my Mother, Clara Agnes Braaten

On June 25, 1922 at 7:10 pm we left Union Station in Minneapolis. A few of our friends and relatives saw us off. The evening was beautiful and we were both in good humor and health.

June 26. We arrived in Chicago 8 o'clock in the morning. Unused to going to bed on a train we did not sleep much, and we were afraid that Torstein, who had the upper berth, would roll out of bed on the floor. Our first impression of Chicago was not very favorable. The Union Station was one of the dirtiest places in the city. All we accomplished was a trip to Montgomery Ward and bought a little lunch. We left Chicago at 5:30pm that same day on one of the fastest trains speeding non-stop to New York.

June 27. We are to arrive in New York tonight. We had a good night's rest. When we awoke we saw a different lay of the land, high hills with towns close together, small patches of fields and gardens, and very poor buildings. We enjoyed having breakfast in our berth. At 8:30am as we were winding up the mountains, we came to a wonderful bend called Horseshoe Curve, which wound around a great canyon. This is the grandest scenery I have ever seen in the USA. It is a little foretaste of what we hope to see when we come to Norway. We arrived in New York at 5:30pm, called up Rev. Eikjarud at the Immigrant Home and were met by one of the workers. We took our first ride on the underground street car.

June 28. We had a good rest last night. We took a walk down town on the Broadway and then rode an elevator to the top of the Woolworth Building. After that we took a sightseeing tour around the city.

June 29. We went to the docks in Brooklyn both forenoon and afternoon. Eikjarud took us to the new Immigrant Home which our church was just about to buy. In the evening we took the ferry to see the Statue of Liberty. It's a wonderful piece of art, presented to America by France. We climbed up half-way.

June 30. We left Brooklyn on board the Stavangerfjord at noon. As the boat began to move, the band played the Star Spangled Banner. What a strange feeling to leave our homeland for a foreign land like Madagascar. It was as if our heart strings were being broken.

The day was beautiful and the ocean was quiet. The boat is said to be one of the finest modern ocean liners crossing the Atlantic Ocean. The boat began to lift at supper time so I did not feel so well. On Saturday and Sunday we had very fine weather. Services were held on Sunday morning, led by Rev. Njaa from Northwood, North Dakota. (Torstein wants dinner as soon as possible; Clara wants to sleep only once in awhile, that is, all the time).

July 4. We cannot realize it's the fourth of July. A divine service was held in the morning. There was some kind of entertainment all day long.

July 8. The sea was more quiet today than it has been since we left New York. We are very well and enjoying the trip.

July 9. We passed the Shetland Islands and came into the North Sea about midnight. We noticed the ship began to pitch more but still had nice weather. About 1 o'clock am we stopped and took a pilot on board. From then on we went at slow speed into the Bergen fjord. Torstein got up at 2 o'clock am to see land and get a first glimpse of his home country which he had not seen for thirteen years. I slept until the usual time and wasn't very excited about it. On both sides of the fjord we could see neat fishermen's homes dotting the barren cliffs, and we could see beautiful little gardens around the houses and green patches with white fences around them.

We landed at the pier of Bergen at 4 o'clock in the morning. We had our passports and landing cards inspected. At 5am we had breakfast and then stepped ashore with our suit cases and went for the mission hotel. Having reserved a room for the night we went downtown to see the historical places and nature sceneries. First we went to see Haakon's Halle and Hanseatic Museum. Then we took a ride on the Flörbanen which took us to the top of the mountain where we got a bird's eye view of the whole city.

Bergen lives up to its reputation. We've been tramping around in the rain all the time. I had to buy a pair of rubbers into which I had to stick cotton because they were so wide that otherwise it was impossible to wear them. About 2:00pm we were tired of tramping around town on account of the constant rain. So we went home to our lodging in the Mission Hotel where I am now writing these memoirs. We had found a bakery where we bought some rolls and cheese.

We left Bergen on Tuesday at 8:30am in a third class car. The trip from Bergen to Christiania (now named Oslo) was very interesting and scenic. We passed through 178 tunnels, Grav-halsen being the longest, 5,311 meters in length. The snow was still lying on the mountain tops. Coming up to Finse the ground was covered with snow. Boy, was it cold. We arrived in Christiania 10:30pm. Torstein's friend, Mr. Seierstad, met us. He had arranged a room for us at the Bible School. The next day we went to the docks to get our baggage inspected. Then we took a walk around the park around the Royal Palace. We remembered the big dish of ice cream that we tried so hard to find in Christiania. We enjoyed our room at the Bible School; it was new and everything was so clean.

On Thursday we took a train from Christiania to Noragutu, Telemarken. We were on our way to Akerhus where Mr. Rugtveit, Torstein's brother-in-law, met us with a one-horse cart and took us to his home. Here was Ingeborg, Torstein's sister, with her five children. Aunt Ingeborg also came there to see us.

July 21. We took a boat to Dalen to see the mountains. We were on this little steamer for twelve hours. The day was wonderful and beautiful, as we sailed along small streams with mountains on both sides, with some places barely wide enough for our boat to pass through. We also went through several locks[1] and saw some beautiful water falls. After we arrived in Dalen we went to Hotel Bandak. Dalen lies in a very narrow valley; many of its houses are built on the sides of the mountain.

The next day we started out for a mountain hike toward Hawkeli Sater. How we would rather have taken a sightseeing bus but we could not afford it. The scenery was most wonderful, with small mountain streams flowing so gently toward the large streams that rushed along more rapidly. After walking for three hours we climbed up the mountain side and ate our lunch. Then we took the journey back down to Bö, which is the small town close to the farm where the Braaten family lived and worked.

On Sunday we hired a car which took us to the church in Bö where Torstein was confirmed and which he attended as a boy. Since there were no services at the time we spent the time looking at the new and old church buildings and the graveyard where Torstein's father and mother are buried. In the evening we went for a dip in the lake.

July 25. Our trip to Dalen was wonderful. We looked forward to our second trip to Rjukan with great expectation, when we would come to the famous mountain of Gausta. However, the weather was unfavorable and the trip to Gausta was strenuous. We started out in the morning, having prepared eats for the day. After having climbed for two hours, we arrived to the top of the mountain. What a huge stone pile, just a mass of big rocks and boulders. In places we could not see a sign of a path. Torstein hopped like a rabbit between the big boulders but I had to crawl. At seven o'clock we finally arrived at the three room stone house where we could get lodging for the night. Boy, was it cold up there. After supper we went still higher up to the very highest peak. Torstein went way up but I could not manage it — too dangerous for me. It was

---

[1] A lock is an enclosed chamber in a canal with gates at each end, for raising or lowering vessels from one level to another by admitting or releasing water. We went through many of them on our various trips by boat in Norway.

a peculiar feeling to be so high above everything else; it felt as if we were on dangerous ground.

The next morning was very foggy so we could see nothing. Too bad! Then we began our descent. A little while after we left it began to rain, and it drizzled all day long. Terrible! The descent was harder than the ascent. It seemed impossible for me, but eventually we made it all the way down. What a sight we must have been. The children in the street followed us to get a good look. I was dressed in Torstein's black coat and black gymnasium bloomers, and I wore a blue dress hat that was as soaked as it could be. Torstein walked ahead with a knapsack on his back. I was too tired to keep up. He was cross and out of patience. I was simply "all in," but could not help but laugh at the scene, as we were walking down the street of Rjukan that evening. It was good to get to a hotel, a little dinky place, where we could change our clothes and get something to eat.

The panorama from the top of Gausta was disappointing and the accommodations in Rjukan were very simple, yet expensive. All these things combined made a rather unfavorable impression on us, and so we are glad that the tour has come to an end.

July 29. We took a boat to Bergen to visit Hans Braaten, Torstein's oldest brother, and his family. Hans was given the family farm when his parents died, since the custom was that the eldest son inherits the farm. We stayed here several days. Hans had lost the farm some years before for some reason.

August 2. We left for Bö to visit Torstein's boyhood friends, his old family home, and the "Sater," the summer mountain home where the boys tended the sheep. First, we visited Sigurd Sönstebö, Torstein's best friend, and remained there for two nights. Then Sönstebö took us to Skjeldbred by horse and buggy and stayed there over night. Gunhild and Hans were very kind. She went with us the next morning to Li Fjeld by way of the old Braaten home where we stopped for a few minutes to take a look at the place. It lies at the farthest end of the valley, between the wilds of the mountains. What a struggle it must have been to carry all the provisions such a long way on such a road. It is remarkable that three boys — Olaf, Kittel, and Torstein — from this little mountain home left for America, worked their way through college and seminary, and all became missionaries. Then we proceeded to the Sater, the old mountain home, where Sigurd Sönstebö and his sister had gone ahead to make it comfortable for us. Here we could rest in peace and quietness. We were surrounded by high mountains, a brook was running noisily below, and the cattle were grazing on the mountain slopes.

We picked blue berries and cooked. We enjoyed the french toast. Every evening Torstein went across the valley for a quart of sour cream, the most wonderful we ever tasted. These few days I enjoyed more than anything else in Norway.

August 11. In the morning we said goodbye to Sigurd and his sister and walked down the mountain. We got terribly tired, so we hired the first car we could get to take us to the Rugtveits. Mrs. Rugtveit was Torstein's sister Ingeborg. Hans Braaten and his wife came to see us. Early Monday we bade Rugtveits farewell. Little did we think that Ingeborg would pass away before we could meet again. (She passed away the spring of 1930). We boarded a little steamer to Heistad, Eidanger, to visit Torstein's aunt Ingeborg, and had a short but very nice visit.

August 17. We left Heistad for Christiania (Oslo) where we secured a room at the Bible School. Several days later we took a train from Ost Banen to Arneberg, Solor, to visit my mother's and father's homes and some of my relatives. Nearing Arneberg a strange man wanted to talk to me. I became suspicious. I knew he could tell that we were Americans, so I thought maybe he was looking for a chance to pick pocket us. We finally learned that the man was uncle Anton — a good joke on me! We rode to his home in a carriage. This was Saturday.

On Sunday two of my uncles, Haakon and Ole, and a cousin of my mother came over to get acquainted with their American niece and cousin. We remained at uncle Anton's home until Thursday. One day we took a bath in the river. I remember the *"römmegröt"* (a Norwegian pudding) auntie made for us. I got an awful ache in my "tummy."

August 24. Uncle Haakon Ostmoe[2] came to get us on Thursday noon. He had a nice home. And how they waited on us. Here I saw my mother's birthplace. On Saturday Oyvind took us for a ride to Aasa to see my father's birthplace, Titerud. It still goes by that name. The same buildings were still standing, but there was a new home on the place. Took two pictures of it. How I wish father could have been along! In the afternoon we were invited to Uncle Ole's for dinner. Uncle Ole and wife had retired from farming and were living in a small house next to the big one, where his son lived.

On Thursday we took the train to Elverum; Uncle Haakon accompanied us to visit Uncle Peder's wife and children. Uncle Peder had been dead for many years. They met us and took us by car to their beautiful home on the shore of the Glommen River. Neither one of us had ever lived in luxury but here we got a good taste of it. The house was richly furnished, and they had a seven passenger car. The next day they took us for a ride to Hamar through the wealthy part of Hedemarken. The farmers looked to be wealthy. Such large buildings, main house and barns, I have not seen the like in America. The valley of Glommen was very wide with islands and arms of the river flowing between. Uncle Eberhart had a store and also had a very nice home. They had five boys at home, and their only girl was away. On Sunday we went up on the hill to have a view over the valley. Koppang lies way up in the mountains with Koppang Islands below. There seemed to be only wealth in the Storelvedalen area.

September 3. We took the train back to Christiania on Sunday morning. On Monday we tended to business matters. In the evening we went to the National Theater to see *"Brand,"* a play by Henrik Ibsen. Wednesday we went sight seeing: the two Viking ships, two museums, a trip to Ekeberg and also to Folks museum in Bygdö. This is a large museum with collections from all the "Bygds" in Norway — old churches and other houses with furniture. After dinner we went to Vär Frelsers' gravlund, a cemetery in Oslo, to see the statues of the most famous

---

[2] Ostmoe is the family name of mother's mother. Her name was Martha Karen Ostmoe. She married Martin Titrud, my mother's father.

persons in Norway, such as Ibsen, Björnson, Welhaven, Jonas Lie, Ivar Aasen, etc. In this beautiful cemetery we sat for awhile to enjoy the surrounding scenery, trees and flowers while the autumn sun was smiling down upon us. The events of the day ended in the National Theater where we saw the well known play by Holberg, "*Erasmus Montanus.*"

September 8. This is Friday, the day we set out for Paris, France. Part of the time was taken up with those tedious details, inevitable when one is to set out on a longer trip. I was nervous when I had to see a doctor about a skin disease I had on my arms. After that I was to meet Torstein down by the dock at a certain time. I had no idea where I was to go to get there. But I got there!

We left Christiania at noon sharp. Now while we are rocking on the billows, we pause here to look back upon our short stay in Norway with fond recollections. We have just said goodbye to Norway for a long time, maybe forever. But the memories will always remain with us as long as we live. We had a last look at the rugged cliffs just as they were about to pass out of sight. The sun came through the clouds on the horizon, as if to enhance the memory of Norway and inscribe it with indelible character on our minds.

At supper time I got sea sick and had to hurry to bed. Torstein had lobster and also got sea sick. The little coast steamer sure did roll. The next two days, September 9 and 10, are blank because we were so sea sick. On September 11 we stepped off the ship in Antwerp, Belgium, and passed through customs with no trouble whatsoever. The captain secured a taxi for us and a wagon for our baggage. But we had no Belgian money so we exchanged a $10 bill on the way to the train station. We finally arrived at the station, got our baggage checked, bought a few sandwiches, and got on the train safely bound for Paris.

As we road through Belgium we noticed that there was a continuous city most all the way, with large factories saturating the air with coal dust. Having come through Belgium into France, we came into the war stricken country (from World War I). Cities and towns and farms were in ruins. The fields were torn up, the trees shot to pieces. A great deal of construction had been done already, but there are towns where no reconstruction had been started at all.

We arrived in Paris the same evening. Here we began to realize how helpless we were in a foreign country, not knowing a word of the language. We soon visited some of the famous places in Paris — Versailles, Cluny Cloister, Musée de Victor Hugo, Chateau de Vincennes, La Conciergerie et Palais de Justice, Musée des Arts Decoratifs. We enjoyed our French language classes under Miss Le Hoc. We will always remember her.

May 17, 1923. We celebrated this special day for Norway by having dinner at Hotel Dagmar with Sister Anna and the Norwegian missionaries. At 4 o'clock we had coffee with Sister Hanna Baarstad together with all the Norwegian girls.

We had many interesting experiences in Paris. We also remember the many cozy hours we had together with Sister Anna at Hotel Dagmar. We made many excursions with the students which were very interesting and instructive. We left Paris May 18 for Marseilles and enjoyed the trip very much. The scenery was beautiful the whole way. The vegetation in France is luxurious. The railroad follows along the river with mountains in the background. On May 19 we visited the quai of Messageries Maritimes and also the ancient chateau. What a horrible history that castle has. The cold bare dungeons where many poor souls suffered agony until their frail bodies gasped their last breath. We were in Marseilles for five days, May 19-24.

On the 24th at 4 o'clock we left for Madagascar on the Azay-le-Rideau, a steamer named after a famous chateau. The day was beautiful, the sea very calm, and the air quite warm. We shared a cabin with Sister Anna. Our hope is that we may have a fine voyage all the way but that is more than we can expect. On May 29 we reached Port Said, 1300 miles from Marseilles, and remained there all day while they loaded coal. On May 30 we sailed through the Suez Canal all night and entered the Red Sea at noon. It was interesting to see the sandy deserts along the canal and the Red Sea. It was nice and cool on deck all day so I made use of my woolen scarf at times. The sky was hazy from the heat of the sun on the bright sand. Among the interesting things to see on the boat was a band of soldiers, about 300 in all. Their deck was right outside our dining room. The different smells from their deck did not increase our appetite one bit. There was also an Abyssinian priest who with all his paraphernalia ate and slept on deck with his two slaves. We are 1282 miles from Djibouti, our next stop.

Torstein is writing the following. There are many Malagasy soldiers on board. One of them died today and was lowered into the Red Sea. We don't know if he was a Christian; at least we didn't notice any Christian burial ceremony. It is June 2 today, exactly one year since we were married. As a gift in honor of our anniversary Clara is now mending my shirts.

Last night it got too hot for Sister Anna and Clara to sleep in the cabin, so they went on deck and slept there until the washwoman turned the hose on them. I didn't think it was too warm so I stayed in the cabin.

Today another soldier died and rests now on the bottom of the sea. Poor soldiers, they are not given much comfort. I can't help thinking that when they are good enough to be soldiers for France, the government ought to treat them as human beings and not place them in the pit like animals.

Since yesterday noon we have made 334 miles, the most mileage since we started. Azay-le-Rideau is a very good boat. We have good service and everything is all right, only a little warm. Today is the warmest we have had. Just now we are seeing twelve small islands called the Twelve Apostles. However, there isn't much apostolic about them. They look like the straw stacks after threshing on the North Dakota prairie.

June 3. There are 1870 miles from Djibouti to Mombasa. It is very warm today, but we are feeling fairly well. Yesterday we stopped at Djibouti for 13 hours. At this port we saw the expert brownie swimmers. Some of them jumped from the upper deck into the sea and then swam underneath the boat and came up on the other side.

June 10. We will arrive in Mombasa in a few hours and there we will step ashore in order to assure ourselves that the earth is solid. There has not been much solid for us for some days, neither us nor around us. There has been a blank in our diary for some days now. As soon as we came into the Indian Ocean, it showed its bad temper and made all three of us sick. We offered all we had to the sea gods, but they looked for more and kept us prostrated till yesterday. Today we are feeling fairly well. But the sea god does not seem to be satisfied yet, because we are having a high wind and it rains every once in a while.

(Torsetin is still writing this part of the diary). We arrived in Zanzibar and the boat has been lying idle. We were quite out of whack when we arrived, so we were really glad to be in port for a while. It did not take us long, however, to recuperate. Now we all have a great appetite and stored up strength for the rest of the voyage. Zanzibar looks very beautiful from the sea. One day we stepped ashore to see the town at closer range. We found it very interesting. The streets are very narrow and irregular; the houses are made of baked dirt. We had a guide who led us along a big beautiful road with fine trees on both sides and open lawns and playgrounds. When we left the big road the guide led us through the native town which is composed of small huts made of baked dirt and thatched with some kind of grass. In front of the houses the natives were sitting, some of them doing some kind of handiwork, others peeling some kind of roots, and others doing nothing. In addition to people we saw their domestic animals, mostly goats and chickens and the traditional house cat. The animals seemed to be very friendly. In one place we saw a chicken standing on the back of a goat and seemed to feel very much at home there, while the goat on her part didn't mind it at all. In another place we saw some children playing a game that we used to play at home in Norway when we were kids.

(Clara resumes writing the diary). June 17. About 7 o'clock in the morning our boat arrived in the port of Majunga, Madagascar. Here the Malagasy soldiers stepped off and seemed to be very happy coming home. We are to stay here until 5 o'clock this afternoon. We went ashore and had an hour's ride in a *pouse-pousse* for a franc and a half. Here we got a treat by getting two dozen bananas for only 8 cents (in American money) and they were very good.

After leaving Majunga we went to Nossibe and then on to Diego.

Here we went ashore, bags and baggage, to wait for a coastal boat to take us to Fort Dauphin, our final destination. We got comfortable rooms at Hotel des Mines. They told us a boat was to leave for Fort Dauphin in a couple days. Arriving at the hotel we learned that it was to leave in fifteen days. But alas! When the fifteen days were over, the time was changed again and delayed six more days. Then the news came that the scheduled boat was not leaving at all and that we would have to wait until the second of August, a wait of 44 days in all.

The last two weeks we were offered to stay at the home of a French missionary, which we accepted with pleasure. Here we had it nice. Rajosy and Daniel, the servants, were very faithful in waiting on us. The cook succeeded in satisfying our raving appetites. This was ever so much more satisfactory than at the hotel, where we had meat upon meat, yes, four courses of meat per meal, and hardly any vegetables. The last week Rajosy, the cook, prepared just what we liked, such as roast duck, baked pumpkin, fine custard and fried bananas.

While in Diego we went to the French mission church. Though we could not understand the sermons, we enjoyed the singing. Everybody sang as though they were in a choir, very impressive.

August 2. We boarded Bagdad, our coastal steamer, about 4:00pm. We were happy that our stay in Diego had finally come to an end. As soon as we got out of the harbor and into the ocean, the boat began to roll and shake. I kept on vomiting all night and Torstein was sick also. We both felt miserable for days and naturally could not eat. Finally at about 5pm we came to another harbor where the sea was calm. We were able to rest up and began to feel like eating again. When our boat came to the port of Tamatave, we went ashore to see the town and buy some things, jam and crackers, because we are not able to eat what they feed us for breakfast.

Our boat proceeded to sail from port to port, towns like Vatomandry, Manoro, Mananjary, and Farafangana, our last port before reaching Fort Dauphin. The sea is now calm so we can be up and go to the table. On August 16, 1923, we arrived in Fort Dauphin early in the morning. The sea was so rough we had to be taken down from the ship in a basket.

Quite a number of the missionaries met us, among them K. F. Braaten, Torstein's older brother, Trygstad and Pederson. Mrs. Trygstad had a hot breakfast waiting for us. How good everything tasted! Torstein got ready to go with his brother to Manantenina. I could not go so I stayed at Trygstads.

When Torstein returned we began housekeeping. After we were settled, it was time to prepare for our first baby. Agnes Theodora was born on Halloween, All Saints' Day, October 31, at 9:30pm. After eight hours of intense suffering, with two doctors and three nurses doing their utmost to save my life, I was finally relieved. Agnes weighed 3.7 kilos. She was baptized December 9 by Rev. Trygstad. The sponsors were Mrs. K. F. Braaten, Rev. and Mrs. Trygstad, and Rev. and Mrs. Torvik.

We were placed in Manantenina by the Mission Conference. We travelled by Palanquin (called *filanzana* in the Malagasy language), which was the mode of travel in the early days on this mission field. A palanquin is a box-like seat for one passenger, with two poles attached to it and carried on a man's shoulder at each of end of the poles. We arrived safe and sound, but tired and hungry. We left Manambato at 3:15am and made a b-line for Manantenina in one stretch. We arrived at 11am, an 8 hour ride. Then we began to look for something to eat but it took some time. Our baggage arrived safe and sound.

On June 3rd we discovered Agnes' first tooth; she was 7 months and 3 days. After our first year of mission work we left on January 7, 1925 for Fort Dauphin for our annual vacation. We were both well and worked all we could. After our vacation we returned to Manantenina in our *filanzanas*. Little did Agnes know what to do as she entered the house. She now could walk. During the year we had many pleasant visits with Monsieur Bignotti and wife, the French administrator. We will never forget their kindness.

October 6, 1925. We came to Fort Dauphin and went to our vacation house in Lebanon. Lebanon is a peninsula next to Fort Dauphin where the missionaries built summer cottages for use during their summer vacations. Agnes and I stayed on Lebanon while Torstein returned to work at the mission station. Agnes had a skin disease which the doctor claimed was *La Gale Indigene,* a condition that afflicted the natives. I gave her sulphur baths every day and smeared her skin with sulphur salve, but it did not help much. She had this condition for a long time.

On December 25 Arlene was born at 4:45 Christmas morning. She weighed 4.2 kilos. She was baptized on January 24, 1926. Her sponsors were Mr. and Mrs. K. F. Braaten and Sister Anna Gjernes.

At the 1926 annual conference of missionaries we were stationed in Bekily, so now we would get to work in Androy. (Androy is the county north of Tanosy, the county where Fort Dauphin is situated). We left in Tverberg's car while Torstein went on his motorcycle. Little Arlene was only four months old. We left Lebanon at 7:30am and arrived in Behara at 11am. Sister Anna was there to greet us and had some boiled water for us as she promised. All drinking water had to be boiled. We left the next morning for Ambovombe in a *pousse-pousse,* a kind of rickshaw, with eight men taking turns pushing and pulling it. The day's journey was long and tedious. The road was very sandy so going up hill made the speed of our *pousse-pousse* as slow as a turtle, compared to the speed of Torstein's motorcycle more like that of a jack rabbit. Perhaps the time seemed just as long to him as to me, as he spun by me for a good run and then waited until we caught up. We found Androy quite different from what we expected. We would see long stretches of sandy prairie without a tree. Then in places there were shrubs and trees, some quite large, entirely different from what we had ever seen.

Our stay in Ambovombe was interesting. Mrs. Carlson prepared a delicious turkey with raisin dressing for Sunday dinner. We stayed there Saturday and Sunday. We arose at 2 o'clock Monday morning and after a long "*kabary*" (Malagasy for "negotiation") with the Tandroys, we finally got off but then it was already close to 4 o'clock. I had nine big Tandroys for the *pousse-pousse,* so we could move along fast. And did they speed sometimes. Marie Ermine rode with me and she was big and fat. We were not too comfortable. We reached Antanimora at 5 o'clock. This was a hard day. My men were suffering from thirst. Torstein went ahead and returned with water, which made them happy. Pastor Daniela met us with all the help he could offer. The evangelist cooked rice and coffee, but our food container did not arrive before the next morning, so we had to be satisfied with rice and milk. Our beds and bedding did not arrive until late in the evening.

We remained in Antaninmora the next day as we were very tired. We tried to rest up the best we could, but repacking, getting the burdens off and getting ready for the next day just about kept us busy all day. The whole distance from Ambovombe to Antanimora is a dry desert so our burden carriers suffered from thirst. To our surprise we discovered that the only kerosene tin we had became a temptation to its carrier. He had punched several holes in the top to drink from it and got sick so others had to carry his burden.

On Wednesday at 4 o'clock am we left for Bekitro. The road was very difficult; big rocks and stone-filled pits made it almost impassable both for the pousse-pousse and the motorcycle. The people were very primitive. They came around our hut and into it to get a good look at us. We must have looked strange to them, especially Agnes who laughed and sang as if she were by herself. One woman brought us eight nice fresh eggs and a chick, which drew its last breath only a few minutes later. I asked if there were any Christians there, but she said she did not know. Evidently she did not understand what I was talking about. We reached Bekitro at 4:30pm, after five and a half hours of rough riding. Bekitro is one of our mission out-stations. The evangelists met us and helped us with water, etc. We were given two chickens as a gift from the congregation. After such a hard day we were very tired. And there was no boiled water to drink, children crying, everybody hungry, and no one to help us. It was hard to get settled for the night.

We did not start out before 6 o'clock the next morning since we thought we would have a short day, but it took us more than nine hours on a rough road. We were so happy when we reached Bekily, our destination. There was a parade going on when we came into town. People both young and old from every corner, even the French Guard, joined us as we wound our way through town. When I reached the house, the smell of fried chicken and rice met me, and I was so glad someone had taken pity on our poor hungry stomachs. After living on rusks for several days, it was a grand treat to get a home cooked supper.

The station house in Bekily is well planned and beautiful as well. So is the yard and other buildings. After such a weary journey we felt as though we would want to stay here and not take a long journey back to Lebanon. The third evening after we arrived here the whole town with a band and the French Guard came to welcome us. Also the whole congregation came to welcome us and left us twelve chickens and a turkey. In addition we have received thirteen chickens and a turkey. We cannot help but feel that the people are glad to see us come.

June 22. We all piled into the big pousse-pousse and rode to Tranoroa to attend the annual meeting for the Bekily District. Torstein felt so miserable that I did not dare to let him go alone. The road was terrible with long stretches of only rocks and no bridges over the rivers or ravines. After attending one session, Torstein came down with an awful attack of fever so we could not attend many sessions. The children, Agnes and Arlene, felt fine and stood the trip well.

December 28, 1926. We should have left for Fort Dauphin yesterday, but due to the heavy rain the evening before, no men showed up. The men are all here now, thirty eight in number, sleeping on our veranda, so we hope to get off in the morning. We have had a nice Christmas and were able to attend all the church services. Thanks be to God for his loving care from day to day!

December 29. We left Bekily at 4am and reached Antanandava at 9 o'clock. The road was very bad for the motorcycle. Torstein was tired. In the afternoon he took another road which took him in a different direction. The children and I reached Belindo at 5 o'clock, but Torstein did not come until 8 o'clock. In order to join us in Belindo he had to turn back and cross a river, where he got stuck with his cycle. So he came walking, quite exhausted. As he had a flat tire, he had to stay the next morning to repair it and did not get off until 2:30pm. We all arrived at Antanimora at noon and decided to spend the rest of the day and all the next day to rest up. This was New Year's Day, which we did not realize until the pastor told us.

January 2, 1927. We attended church service in the morning and had a nice dinner with the French administrator. We left Antaninmora at 6 in the morning the next day and stopped for lunch under some trees. But it was so hot. The children got sunburned. On January 4 we started off again for Ambovombe. Torstein's motorcycle broke down again. We got to the station house and met missionary Rateaver. To my disappointment Torstein had not yet arrived. He did not come until four hours later, because his cycle had broken down again. He had to work for dear life to get it running again. Oh, how I wish he had never seen that motorcycle. The next day we hope to go to Behara, but we expect bad roads on account of so much rain.

January 5. We left Ambovombe at 5am; the day was very hot for travel. No house to stop in for lunch so we stopped under a tree. Trees are scarce along here. Torstein went ahead as far as the river where we caught up to him before he got across. We reached Behara safely but almost roasted. I was afraid that the children would get sunstroke with the sun beating down on us. It was terrible. We expected that Sister Anna would have already gone to Lebanon, but she was there to greet us and had made supper for us. She has been our standby when we have needed help. Tverberg was also ready with his car to take us the rest of the way to Fort Dauphin. We had hoped to get to Fort Dauphin for dinner, but we were greatly disappointed when the car stopped after going a short distance. There we sat while Torstein came soaring by with his motorcycle, thinking we had stopped for the fun of it. When he heard me yell, he stopped. Rev. Tverberg thought maybe the gas was poor, so they decided that Torstein would go ahead to get some gas. But with his old cycle he barely got to Manambaro. Then he started out on Tverberg's old motorcycle which was no better, so he had to send a man with gas and a few sandwiches as we had no food and very little water with us. Tverberg got some natives to push the car across Mount Tsintsina. We finally reached Ranopiso. There we got a little milk for Arlene. She had had nothing since 7 o'clock in the morning. We finally got some hard boiled eggs and water, for which we were very thankful. What a day! So dry! Poor babies! And poor daddy!

After some dealing we finally got some men to pull us to Manambaro. Torstrein finally came with water and gas. But the old car would not start. It was dead. So Torstein hurried back to Manambaro to hire some men to meet us. They were able to move us along very fast. We reached Manambaro at 8pm, just before dark. Mrs. Tverberg made supper for us, but we were too tired to eat and almost too tired to get ourselves ready for bed.

January 7. Now we have only 4 hours left to Fort Dauphin and we certainly hope to get there without any more trouble. It was not to be. Tverberg got the car started again and after going a ways, it balked on us again. Torstein had to repair his motorcycle before leaving Manambaro, so he was left behind. But he finally came and sped on to Fort Dauphin to get Lovaas and Cartford to take Sister Anna, Agnes, Arlene and me in their sidecars. It did not take long before we arrived in Fort Dauphin. Mrs. Trygstad had a good dinner waiting for us. Words cannot explain how tired we were from this long journey, nor how happy we were that we finally made it to our destination. It was a hard lesson in patience.

March 23. We have had a nice peaceful vacation. The Mission Conference lasted only two weeks. After the Conference we had a whole week of Bible Study under the instruction of Rev. Bjork, a Swedish pastor who travelled as a lecturer. These Bible hours were a great blessing to the missionaries.

April 10. Torstein left for Bekily on his new motorcycle. The rest of us stayed on Lebanon this year, 1927.

September 5. Labor Day! Indeed, it was labor day for me. Folkvard Martinus was born at one o'clock in the afternoon. Sister Anna had been here six weeks waiting for his coming, and long they were. This was the third time Sister Anna and Mrs. K. F. Braaten, my sister in law, helped me during confinement. Folkvard weighed 4 kilos. On September 25 he was baptized by K. F. Braaten. The sponsors were Mrs. Stavaas and Laura Olson. On October 9 I carried Olaf Markus Braaten to baptism, Folkvard's cousin.

On account of Torstein's loss of hearing and poor health, we decided to go home to America in 1928. That is not our wish but when ill health prevents one from accomplishing one's duties, it is better to return home and seek help, and hope to return later. It is April and we have waited two weeks for a boat. Ville de Metz is due here this week and we hope it comes on time. The sea is as calm as a lake. More than two weeks later we boarded a different boat, Imerina. The sea was quite rough, so it was not easy to get on board. The word was that a cyclone was coming. Rateavers were also going home and also Miss Torgeson. The boat left at 10am. We sailed until evening and the storm kept getting worse and worse. The boat rolled a lot and we all got sea sick. Daddy got very sick now; sweats and chills weakened him so he had to stay in bed. The storm continued for four days. The waves were so high that we felt they could swallow up Imerina. I could never imagine that the sea could be so fierce. The water flooded our cabins; our trunks and suit cases rolled from one side to the other. Poor Folkvard stood in his little bed begging to be taken out. I was so sea sick that I vomited every time I lifted my head. Folkvard was seven and half months old and was bottle fed. I tried to cook rice water for him on a small alcohol stove, but that did not work very well. So we tried to get some from the kitchen but that was so dirty. Oh, such terrible service on Imerina. The napkins looked like my floor rags. The Malagasy servants were as careless and dirty as could be. Mr. Grouch, as we called the steward, was a demon, to say the least.

The fourth evening of the storm after we had gone to bed, fire broke out in the kitchen and the smoke was pouring into Miss Torgeson's cabin. Was this to be the end of all of us? It seemed as if it could be. But the fire was killed, and again we had hope that we would be saved. These hours of fear brought us closer to our Heavenly Father who has all power in His hands. If it would be His will that we should perish out there on the fierce ocean, we were prepared to leave this life. And so we waited for the sea to become more calm or still more fierce.

April 23. Finally at 4pm we arrived at Farafangana. For five days we remained in this harbor. The first two days they could not load or unload. Rateaver stepped off the boat sliding down a rope. We are supposed to leave this afternoon at 4pm. We are always happy to hear the bell ring for "*départ.*"

April 29. We arrived in Manakara this morning. There is a big German boat in the harbor. On May 1 we left for Mananjary and arrived around 4pm. On the way we saw Ville de Djebouti stranded. On May 7 we arrived in Tamatave. We went to Hotel de Place, a fine place, and rented a room for our baggage for 12 francs per day, and got ready to go to Tananarive, the capitol city of Madagascar. On May 8 we got to the station in good time. We had a whole compartment to ourselves. Mr. Pimm met us and took us to a hotel, which was modern, with good rooms and good board. On account of the children it was disagreeable to stay at the hotel, so we asked the Norwegian missionary, Mr. Strand, if it would be possible to stay with one of them. We were welcomed to Isoraka by Fröken Garpestad and Rev. and Mrs. Skarpaas. How happy we were to get into a home where good home cooked food was served. Their kindness was greatly appreciated.

May 24. Papa left for Antsirabe, Fianarantsoa, and Ambalavao. Today Miss Torgeson left for Tamatave. June 2 is our 6th wedding anniversary. Daddy returned from his trip. On June 3 we had an ice cream party. Mrs. Skarpaas and I made a very good cake. It was a real treat. We had a very good time with these folks. Mrs. Skarpaas is a real Charlie Chaplin.

Tananarive is quite an interesting city. It is very hilly and the houses are built up the sides in steps. The market place is also interesting. On June 10 we left for Tamatave. On June 11 we got orders to get vaccinated against the plague which is raging in Madagascar. We all hurried down to the doctor to get inoculated. Arlene and Folkvard escaped from it.

Daddy hurried gown to the dock with all our baggage, but they refused to take it on board that day. That night it rained so we were quite worried about it. But it was in good shape the next day. Rateavers arrived from Tamatave in the last minute. On June 13 we all boarded the ship, General Voyron. The food was good and everything very clean. Our stewardess is very nice and accommodating.

June 15. We arrived at Antalaha this morning and left in the evening. Daddy got sea sick and vomited out his teeth. *Quel Malheur*! With a whole month ahead of us on French food and no teeth? Fortunately he found his second set in one of the trunks.

June 16. We arrived in Diego today and were on deck all day as our cabins were closed. We left in the evening of June 17. The whole ship was covered with coal dust, so we had to stay in our cabins all day in spite of the heat. It was quite windy and rough. Papa went on deck and lost his cap in the ocean. What next? On June 19 we arrived in Majunga and stayed two days. Everybody went on shore except me and the children. On June 21 we came to the island of Mayotte, the first port after leaving Madagascar. On this part of our journey we went to Daresalem, then to Zanzibar and Mombassa, and it took five days crossing the Arabian Sea. Next we went to Aden, Arabia and Djibouti on our way to the Red Sea. From July 7 to 11 we were on the Mediterranean Sea. Fine sailing and everybody is well. On July 12 we arrived in Marseille and rented a fine room at Hotel Genève. We bought some hats and then proceeded to Paris on July 14, the French national holiday. So when we got to Paris we had a hard time to get a taxi to take us to the hotel. We were so tired and dirty that we had to take a bath even though it was past midnight. On July 15 we rested all day. We bought tickets for the Aquitania and hope to leave in a week. In the meantime we had to buy coats and other pieces of clothing.

On July 21 we left for Cherbourg and arrived there at 3pm. The next day we were sailing along all day. Daddy lost his hat. Where can it be? He hunted all day but couldn't find it. The food is delicious, luxurious. What a treat to get apples, ice cream, pie, etc. The service is excellent but the cabin is nothing special. Finally this afternoon daddy got his hat back. If he had not made such a fuss about it, he would never have seen it again.

The voyage across the Atlantic Ocean was wonderful for us. It was exciting getting to New York. The long wait with the little ones was tiresome. Folkvard was fussy and did not feel good. But we got through the inspection all right. The Norway House took care of us. Rev. and Mrs. Bjerke were very kind. We stayed in New York one day in order to transfer our baggage to the railway station. In Chicago we went to the Deaconess Hospital. Folkvard took sick again and cried throughout the night. We remained there one day on account of him. Then we proceeded to Minneapolis on August 1. We called up Augusta, my sister. She was very surprised. We took a taxi to her house. It seemed good to be back on ground and meet our beloved ones again. Pretty soon Olga, my younger sister, came too. We rented a little cottage on Buford Avenue, St. Paul, where we stayed until April 1, 1929.

On January 3, 5am, Carl Edward was born. He weighted 12 pounds, an immense baby. Folkvard had taken sick on Christmas Eve, with a temperature of 106 degrees. Dr. Bentley was called and pronounced it scarlet fever. Then he came down with whooping cough, and Agnes and Arlene got it shortly thereafter. We were placed under quarantine for scarlet fever and whooping cough when the time for the baby's arrival came. No nurse could be had on account of so much sickness in the cities. But the doctor and daddy got busy and everything went fine. The second day we got a nurse. Carl was baptized February 3; the sponsors were Mrs. Hjort, Clarence and Olga Ryberg, and the pastor was Dr. Malmin of St. Anthony Park Lutheran Church. This was a hard winter for us. The children were very sick with the whooping cough. Folkvard was simply a skeleton when spring came.

On April 1 we moved to our own home on 1435 Grantham St. Here we had it comfortable. In the later part of April daddy had an operation for appendicitis. That summer we spent two weeks on Lake Independence. Blanche spent one week with us. That summer was otherwise a dull time for me. Agnes began to attend school. Olga's and Augusta's families drove over frequently and we enjoyed their visits. Daddy was out almost every Sunday during the summer preaching in some congregation, so I was alone most Sundays.

After much consideration we decided to return to Madagascar. Our hearts yearned more and more to return to our work there. On the first of April I had two operations which were successful. Then it was time to pack and to store all our furniture before June 1. Most of my sewing was done, but I had planned to do much more. We sold our home to J. I. Anderson and went to stay at Olga's until it was time to leave America.

We drove to Battle Creek to visit Olaf Braaten and his family. Olaf was Torstein's older brother who had been a missionary in China.

On June 27, 1930 we left Milwaukee station at 8pm. Mr. and Mrs. Dalland, Betsy Severson and son Myron, Emma, Augusta and Olga and families, and Rev. Höverstad were there at the station to see us off. It was always easier for us to meet than to part. It made our hearts sad to say goodbye, but we were also glad to be of use for the furtherance of God's kingdom. We slept well on the train and arrived in Chicago at 8am. We waited at the station for the next train to New work. We left Chicago at 10:45am. We decided to take our meals on the train this time. They proved to be very meagre with a huge price. Never again! The day was quite warm and the kids were restless and uncomfortable. We arrived in New York at 4pm. Rev. Birkelund recommended that we stay at Hotel Chelsea and it was very fine. When one has four small children, one appreciates good accommodations.

On June 30 we boarded S. S. Paris at 6 o'clock in second class. Rateavers travelled back with us also, but they were on third class. We had an inside cabin, so we felt it rather stuffy the first couple of days. We are having wonderful sailing, the sea is calm as a lake, and the food is fairly good. Breakfast is lousy. The boat, however, is clean. It must have an oil burner as there is no soot. I wouldn't want to be in third class. The people are coarse and they do a lot of drinking. It looks dirty over there, no paint on the walls and smelly.

The sunset is wonderful on the ocean. We spent some time playing "Frog," an old time game, typically European. The people are nice and friendly to the children. They call Carl "Dempsey," because he sure is a buster.

We stayed in Paris two weeks. We tried Hotel des Mines, but that is a dump, so we went to Hotel Dagmar again. The cheapest we could get cost 170 francs and 10% service charge. Prices are very high in Paris. We bought things worth over 14,000 francs and still we have only part of the necessary equipment we need for housekeeping. On July 24 we moved on to Marseille and stayed at the Grand Hotel. We have a big fine room for 48 francs per day and we board ourselves, to make it much cheaper. Here too we bought some things for Madagascar. On July 25 we went on board at 3pm. Our baggage arrived safely. Our cabin is very clean and roomy. S. S. Bernardin de St. Pierre is one of the biggest going to Madagascar, an oil burner. Rateavers are traveling in third class. The voyage over the Mediterranean Sea is fine, no sea sickness, good weather, and fairly cool. We slept well.

July 27 we are passing the smoking volcano, Stromboli. We are going so close that we can easily see the homes built upon its sides. A beautiful white castle stands in the midst of the one village. It is interesting to see the black smoke bulging out of the top of Stromboli. At noon we passed Detroit of Messine in Sicily. It is quite a big village with large buildings. On the other side, just opposite, is a large village in Italy. There is only a short distance between Sicily and Italy. On July 28 we passed by Greece. There are huge rocks, like little islands here and there in the ocean. July 31 we arrived at Port Said in the afternoon and left the same evening at 9 o'clock. Port Said is large with many beautiful buildings. Here the boat got a new supply of oil. During the night we went through the Suez Canal. The night was very cool. We did not reach Suez until afternoon the new day. The boat went very slowly through the canal. The only vegetation to be seen are the trees planted along the canal. From time to time we see a station where a watchman lives. The air is hazy from the bright sunshine on the sand. It is very hot, 90 degrees in our cabin. Yet, our cabin is the coolest place; it is very hot on deck. I enjoy the scenery along here, though it is very barren.

It is August 1 and we have left Suez. Both daddy and I have to eat with the children and it happens most of the time that we are through with our meal by the time the boat leaves the harbor. At that time the grown ups go down and we have the whole deck to ourselves. We can enjoy the twilight in peace. It was 90 degrees in our cabin so we slept on deck. We went down to our cabin and everybody had a sponge bath. Then daddy discovered he had left his glasses on deck. When he returned to get them, they were gone. Someone must have picked them up, for it seems impossible for them to have fallen overboard. It seems to get hotter each day, 94 degrees in our cabin and even hotter on deck. The children are all fine, but Carl is getting prickly heat. Daddy is under the weather. We all slept on deck. The man who works in the engine room died from heat stroke. In third class where the Rateavers are there is an awful commotion. There are many soldiers in fourth class.

On August 6 we got to Djibouti; it is 96 degrees in our cabin. We will reach Aden this afternoon. We sent a letter to Dr. Fjeldstad for a pair of glasses.

When we crossed the equator there was a great excitement, especially for those crossing for the first time. There were games all afternoon. August 12 and 13 we went from Mombassa to Zanzibar. Here many Arabs came on board with all kinds of novelties. This evening we stop at Daresalem, and many are getting off here. We won't miss them. One of these rascals stole daddy's felt hat.

We stopped in a number of places, including Arjaon, Majunga, Nose Bé, Diego on our way to Tamatave, our last port on this boat. When we got to Tamatave we looked for the best way to get to Fort Dauphin. To go by sea we heard we would have to wait 29 days for a boat. We also heard that it was now possible to travel by automobile from Tananarive to Fort Dauphin. We telegrammed Fort Dauphin and asked what we should do. They wrote back, hire a car. We had to wait three days in Tamatave before we could get our baggage through customs. We took a train to Tananarive. The train stops quite often and the people get off to buy fruits or water. Everybody likes Tananarive, but we did not want to stay there any longer than necessary. We hired a car and then prepared to drive over a thousand kilometers to Fort Dauphin. To make this journey with small children is not easy. After what seemed like a long and tedious journey we finally reached Fort Dauphin on September 5, Folkvard's birthday. We were so happy to see our missionary friends and the natives we learned to know during our first term. The work is growing and the opportunities are many. It continues to be our hope and prayer that the Lord may use us for the furtherance of His kingdom among the Malagasy people.

We had to wait a whole month for our baggage to arrive. We stayed with the Braatens, as there was no house for us. The 3rd of October we left for Ambovombe in our new Amilcar. This was quite a different way of traveling from what we were used to. The roads are splendid. We heard that there is a serious famine in Androy. Hundreds are dying from lack of food. The most pitiful sights of human beings one can imagine come begging for food. We remained in Ambovombe until January 9. Agnes came from school in Fort Dauphin and spent Christmas with us, so we were not in a hurry to go to Lebanon. There was no house for us there anyway. The rainy season came so we were forced to stay longer than we planned. When we did finally get to Lebanon, we had to get busy to get the house in shape so we could live in it. At the Conference we were placed in Bekily, where we had worked before, like home coming.

In 1931 we had *Isan-Taona* in Tsivory which we missionaries from Bekily looked for to attend. *Isan-Taona* is Malgasy for Annual Conference. When our folks from Bekily got half way, there was a big rain, not so pleasant for them on the road, but still a big blessing for the parched ground. On account of the rain we were in doubt whether we could cross the rivers in our car, but after three and a half hours we were able to cross safely all the rivers and brooks. When the Bekily folks, 76 in number, approached the town, the Tsivory folks went out to greet them and escorted them to the new complex which the mission had bought. There the host welcomed the visitors and treated them to tea and cakes and gave them half an ox for their meat.

The Convention opened with divine services conducted by Pastor Albert. He preached on the text John 4: 24, which dwelt on the necessity of prayer when doing the Lord's work. The afternoon session was set aside for discussion. Pastor Peter introduced the theme, "The fields are white unto harvest," based on John 4: 35. During the discussion we were reminded of the privilege and the responsibility we as Christians have in bringing in the sheaves while it is still day. The forenoon of the following day was also devoted to discussion. The afternoon and evening sessions were set aside for programs presented by the various societies. One interesting feature of the meeting was the large number of children present, at least 250 of them. The pews were all occupied by the adults so the children had to squat on the floor. The future lies with the children, so I venture to say that Tsivory has a promising future.

One catechist brought with him thirty Tandroys at his own expense. Eleven of them were admitted to the church through holy baptism. Sunday was the last day of the Convention. Torstein preached at the church service and Pastor Peters performed the baptism. Twenty were added to the congregation. In the afternoon we had a communion service and in the evening there were formal talks and singing of hymns. We hope and pray that the seeds sown at this meeting will bear fruit for eternity.

Last night Mrs. Pederson and I cooked chop suey and made sandwiches for a picnic lunch, because we wanted to start out early the next morning for Tamotamo, an out-station 36 kilometers from Tsivory, to have services there. The Tsivory district is very mountainous and the road led us way up over one mountain and into the valley on the other side. After coming up on the highest point, Rev. Peterson stopped his car and showed us where several of his out-stations are located. It was a most picturesque view. The people at Tamotamo did not expect to have services today, because the catechist there was attending a course for catechists. But after ringing the church bell a couple of times, the people came one by one until we had quite a crowd. Rev. Pederson led the service and Braaten gave a brief message. The people were very attentive and seemed to appreciate immensely that the missionaries came to worship with them.

After having had our lunch and an hour's rest, we drove to the river and parked under some big shady trees. Then we sat down on the bank and listened to the song of the birds. In the afternoon we set out for home and it seemed good to be back.

November 19. Papa took me and the children to Fort Dauphin. We went by way of Tsihombe where Hofstad was batching it. We stayed there over night. We had quite a narrow escape in crossing the three rivers as the rains had already begun. But we slipped through safely. Agnes was happy to come home and sleep under the same roof with us. Daddy went back to Bekily and stayed until after Christmas. He had quite a time driving back and forth, since he was having a fever right along and felt miserable.

1932. Time for vacation on Lebanon. Sister Ella was not well and had to leave for France. Little Paul Monson was taken sick suddenly with diphtheria and died after five or six days of illness. We had all hoped and prayed that he might be restored to health, but the Lord seemed to have a different plan. It was a very solemn time for all of us.

On April 5 we left for Bekily with only Folkvard and Carl. This is Arlene's first year away for school. She was a brave girl. We had dinner in Ambovombe with the Stavaases. We arrived in Bekily at 4:30pm. The year was spent attending one conference after the other at our various out-stations such as Beraketa, Tranoroa, and Bekitro.

1933. Papa came to Lebanon the day before New Year's Eve. I gave a party for the two Braaten families; K. F. Braatens were six persons, Kittel, Anna, Conrad, Arndt, Valborg, and Olaf and we were six. I served a big dinner. That year we had a very good missionary conference until the last day. Hallanger's little girl, Anna, became suddenly sick with a serious attack of dysentery and after four days passed away. Freddie also took sick and was in a serious condition, but was eventually restored to health. Then Rev. Hallanger got sick and neither the doctor nor nurses had seen anything like it. Mrs. Rateaver has been sick and in a critical condition for four weeks.

On April 4 we left for Bekily after bringing Agnes and Arlene back to school at the Missionary Childrens' Home in Fort Dauphin. We reached Antanimora at 11:30am. There were Rev. Pederson and Sister Laura. Sister Oline was in bed with fever. Sister Laura put the soup kettle and coffee pot on. Pederson and Sister Laura were quite impatient, having already spent three days there on their way to Tsivory. At 2pm we had to start out again and everything went so well that we rolled into the mission station in Bekily at 5pm. We were so happy and thankful for such a good trip, especially as the rains were so heavy.

In March, 1934, we left for Bekily and this year Folkvard was left behind with his two sisters to attend school in Fort Dauphin. They were all brave. We arrived in Manambaro at 8am for breakfast. Rev. Bjelde had a nice breakfast for us. We arrived in Ambovombe in good time for dinner. At 4:30pm we got to Tsihombe and went to church with Tverbergs. The next morning we started out again for Tranaroa on a new road so we did not know what to expect before we reached Bekily. The road was not good all the way, deep valleys with rough stone bridges. However, we reached Tranaroa before noon. Here the church had a new house for us, but oh, it was too hot in there so we could not rest. The flies were terrible here. This town is noted for its pigs and dogs and our house was close to a group of pig pens that gave off a real strong odor. We finally moved our beds over to the church. Even there it was awfully hot. We stayed here from Thursday noon until Tuesday evening. Papa held services on Good Friday and Easter morning. Six adults were baptized and seven were confirmed. Candidate Samuel is working here. He has gained the favor of the people and has succeeded in getting them to cooperate with him. The Catholics are working against him and call him Lucifer.

Tuesday evening we left for Bekitro and remained there two days. April 9 we arrived in Bekily after ten days of camping. It felt good to get into a nice clean bed again without flees and cockroaches, mosquitoes and flies testing our patience. April 20 we all went to Beraketa for five days. This was the first time I saw the church that Papa had worked so hard to build. With much prayer and planning it now stands all ready and paid for. We hope and pray that this church may be a place where many souls will find their Lord and Savior.

May 12. This past week has been a hard one for Papa. He had two attacks of fever, the most severe he has ever had. Carl came down with fever too, and I came very close to getting it as well, but I managed to fight it off. The doctor has given them three hypos, so we hope that they will not be pestered with fever anymore this year.

July 15. Papa left early this morning to have services in Bekitro in the morning and in Tranaroa in the afternoon. Pastor Albert and Antoinette went with him as they are moving to Fort Dauphin. Papa attended the Pastoral Conference in Fort Dauphin and returned with the children, Agnes, Arlene, and Fokvard, along with their grade school teachers, Miss Rörstad and Miss Gulbrandson, who will spend their vacation with us.

We have been working hard to clean up the house, painted all the rooms both upstairs and downstairs and waxed all the floors. When they all returned to school, I went with them.

September 28. We dedicated a church in Beraketa. Rev. Monson, the mission Superintendent, Sister Oline and Pastor Daniela were with us as well. The church is well built and so are the furnishings. After spending three days in Beraketa we left for Fort Dauphin. The rains had already begun, so we barely got across the Merarandrana river. We arrived safely, so we had one day to rest up before the Childrens' Christmas program. How our children rejoiced to have us home again. The Christmas vacation did not turn out as we expected. All except for me were in bed with the flu with high temperature. They were able to get over it without any doctor.

1935. We are at the opening of another year. Everyone is well on this vacation at Lebanon. I am terribly busy getting all four children ready for school. Carl also begins school this year. We had a birthday party for him on January 3.

April 5. We left the the children at the M. C. Home last night. This morning we left for Behara and Sister Mette had dinner prepared for us. Mrs. Rateaver took us for a walk around town, very dilapidated. There has been a huge famine in this area, so many are starving.

April 6. We went on to Ambovombe where Samuel is to be ordained. Papa took sick so he could not even go to church. Three days later we went on to Antanimora and arrived in Bekily on April 11.

Papa has had frequent bouts of dysentery. He received 16 hypos of emetine and 2 of Novar. He became so weak and lost 6 kilos. All of this interfered with his work.

December 14. I went to Fort Dauphin in Felli's truck. We left Bekily at noon and came to the Mandrare river where we waited for 5 hours before we got across. Now it was night, so I had to sleep in a native hut with no supper or bedding for my bed. I could not rest well, so I was happy to start for Fort Dauphin at 4 o'clock in the morning. We got there when the children just had breakfast. They were so happy to see me and came running as fast as they could. Meanwhile Papa spent Christmas alone in Beraketa and came here three days later.

1936. The beginning of a new year, time for the missionary conference. Papa preached and led the whole service with communion. His text was about the race which we must run in order to attain the goal. Everybody is well and the weather is so beautiful. We have so much to be thankful for. God has richly blessed us in every way. And now He has led us into another year of service. May He be permitted to use us for the furtherance of His kingdom here in Madagascar.

We returned to our work in Bekily early in April. This will be our eighth year working at this mission station. We got the bad news that Hallanger's little girl, Eunice, died on the boat after they left for America.

1937. We had vacation on Lebanon as usual. Alene had an attack of fever, but got over it. Leif Stolee was sick with dysentery. James Stolee also got sick. I have not been writing many entries in my diary this year. This is our last year in Bekily. We can hardly realize that more than seven years have passed since we came here. We have had a good year in many respects, but with very little rain the crops have failed and famine has been severe.

One outstanding event this year was the reception of a gift 50,000 francs for a new church here in Bekily. So papa has been gathering materials, drawing plans and filling out papers for the government. Everything is ready for the next missionary to begin building in the new year. I have not said anything about the beautiful farewell the Bekily folks gave us.

1938. The mission conference in January lasted two weeks. Nothing special happened to report. Feb. 22 is Washington's birthday. The missionaries in Lebanon gathered at Norlies' cottage. We enjoyed a good program and a fine supper. It was doubly appreciated because we had had three weeks of rain before, so we found it difficult to pack our trunks. We quit housekeeping four days before our departure. The neighbors all arranged between themselves to have us over for a meal. We received many letters and gifts and good wishes. By February 25 we got through with our packing beautifully and everything was arranged without any nervous exhaustion. Rev. Hofstad took us into town in his fine car for breakfast at Uncles. Then we went down to the pier where all the missionaries were gathered to see us off. The sea had been calm for several days, but this morning it was a little rough. We bade our friends farewell and got into the mission boat. It was quite scary to get on the Ransfjord, our steamer ship. At 11:30am the boat began to move out of the harbor and we had to say goodbye to Madagascar one more time. We enjoyed sailing out from our beloved port. We strained our eyes to see the white sheet of our friends waving us goodbye from Lebanon. We followed the coast of Madagascar the whole day and night and reached Tulear the next morning at 10 o'clock. The sea had been quite rough for Arlene and me, so we were sea sick all afternoon and evening. Even Folkvard had to leave the supper table in a run, so we lost out on a good supper. The dark haired ones in our brood are good sailors and the light haired are not. *Pourquoi?*

Our meals on the Ransfjord are as good as we could wish for. Everything is well made and delicious. Several kinds of cheese, meat and jellies are on the table for breakfast, lunch and supper. Both the noon and evening meals are like dinner so I do not know which is which. The bacon and eggs this morning struck a good nerve and oh was that a good feeling. We had breakfast at a quarter of eight, so our appetites were sharp. This morning the sea is so calm as we are lying in the Tulear harbor; we are sure to enjoy our dinner.

Miss Sivesind and our family are the only passengers. We have the most beautiful cabins we have ever had on any boat. They far surpass the second class cabins we had on the big boats crossing the Atlantic Ocean. We are very happy to have such fine accommodations. So we are looking forward to a good journey. This afternoon we got a big canoe with an outrigger on it, so we went ashore to visit the Norwegian missionaries. Rev. Anderson met us in his fine car and took us to his home where the coffee table stood ready for us in good Norwegian style. Rev. and Mrs. Berge, Rev. and Mrs. Soveraas, and Miss Wersland came also, so we were a whole company. They served waffles, cakes, and coffee. After that they took us for a ride around town and we were surprised to see how large and beautiful the town of Tulear is. They invited us, yes, even insisted that we stay over and attend church services with them the next morning, which we were glad to accept. But I had a big pang in my heart because I remembered I had not locked my trunk in my cabin. It turned out all right; we had a nice visit and came back on the boat safely. We left Tulear February 29, 4:30pm on Sunday. We have had fine sailing on our way to Morombe. Here we are to load 700 tons of cargo. Our next stop is Morondava. We were all treated to take a tour through the engine room and to see the enormous machinery. The food served on the boat continues to be splendid — bacon and eggs, cheeses, meats, jellies, soups, fish and potatoes, a real smorgasbord every meal. Very good.

The journey from Fort Dauphin to Bordeaux, France, took the whole month of March. We got sea sick from time to time when the sea was rough. Captain Thon told us that we traveled over 8000 miles to get to France. From Bordeaux we took the train to Paris. It is spring in France now, the fruit trees are in full bloom, the leaves on the trees are so fresh and the grass on the pastures so green. Farmers are sowing and plowing. The farmers use oxen and horses for plowing, no tractors. We see very few cars on the country roads. The farms are very small and the cattle shed is right next to the walls of the house. The farmers are using very primitive implements, but in spite of that they seem to be making a good living.

We took the taxi to Hotel Trevise where we got a room; we got out for some meals and some we make on our own. We visited the following places: Louvre, Jardin des Tuileries, Place de la Concorde, Sacre Coeur, Musée de Cluny, Pantheon, Église St. Étienne, Sorbonne University, Jardin de Luxembourg, Napoleon's tomb, Hotel des Invalides, Eiffel Tower, Trocadéra, 1937 Exposition Grounds, Versailles, Rev. Anderson's home for coffee, St. Jean's Church for services, where Rev. Boury preached, to Rev. Rossing's for dinner with all the American missionaries, then to Bois de Boulogne in the afternoon. By the time we had made all these visits, we were tired. Arlene got fever, Folkvard has temperature, Papa's back is all in, Carl has a cold, I the sniffles, and Agnes thinks she has seen enough. Tonight all the American missionaries are invited to

Rev. Boury's for tea at 9 o'clock. Papa has been down to get the tickets to Oslo, by train second class to Antwerp and by Olson's boat second class to Oslo.

April 11. On Saturday morning the 9th we boarded the train for Antwerp. We had a whole compartment to ourselves. The train stopped in Ost-Antwerp and after inquiring if this was Antwerp, we were told "next stop." So we sat down in peace and waited for the next stop. After the train started off again, the conductor came to check up on our tickets, when lo and behold, he said we had already passed by Antwerp and now would have to go along to Rosenthal, Holland. The conductor said we had to pay an extra 358 francs for going the extra distance and return. We were dumbfounded. Could we do anything else but give him what he asked for and follow his advice? When we boarded the train to return, it was a Pullman so we had to pay still more for the privilege. Well, after all this aggravation, we finally made it back to Antwerp. The Olson line agent was there to meet us. He got a taxi for us and took care of our baggage. We wrote a claim against the conductor and wondered if we would every hear more about it.

We found our cabins very small. Everything on second class was very crowded. But the food was good. We boarded Brabant at 5pm Saturday and arrived in Oslo at 10pm Monday night. After arriving in Oslo we went to the Missionary's home where we will be staying, though accommodations are not so convenient. We have been touring all around Oslo but haven't seen anything special. We find prices very high so we have not bought anything.

April 21. At noon we boarded a train for Kirkener, Solor, and took a taxi to Uncle Anton's home. Here Aunt Milla and cousin Olav met us. Uncle Anton died last August 21 of a stroke. He had been cutting wheat all day, and in the evening he complained of being sick in the stomach. During the night he got an attack and died at once without any warning whatever to his wife who was sleeping next to him. His wife, Aunt Milla, is 73 years old and his two children are Odveig and Olav. Olav is a fine boy and is very good to his mother. They have a well built farm with electric lights. It was all built up since last time we were here 16 years ago.

April 25. We hired a car. Aunt Milla and Olav went with us to Arneberg church. We also stopped at the cemetery to see the graves of many of my relatives. Auntie cooked *rommergrod* for us and it was very good. Then we bade Auntie goodbye and had a buggy ride to Uncle Haakon's place called Ommestad. Here Ragnhild and Oivind are running the farm. This place has not changed since we were here in 1922, but we miss Uncle Haakon. He was 76 years old when he died of bladder trouble. We hired a car and rode up to Aasa where the Titrud farm is. It is quite high up and very stony. The old house still stands and no doubt was quite a place in the days of my grandfather. The barn is made of heavy stone walls close to a yard thick. The man on the place now claimed that the barn is also very old. We met an old man, Sjörboten, who knew them all. I wish I could have had a longer talk with him. We saw the old fire place which has cooked many a meal. The land is very hilly, one knoll after the other. I realize now why my father said that he was so glad to get away from there. My father's brother was killed by lightning while he was standing in the doorway, this old man told us. Aunt Milla told me that the Titrud farm was once upon a time a big place. My grandfather became the owner and married a girl who was used to having it swell. When she came to Titrud, she had many servants and lived high. That could not go on for long at Titrud before it would be all eaten up. She then died and grandfather lost everything and finally went to America. Of course, his sons had gone before. Aunt Milla said that my father and Haakon were very able boys and good-looking. Above the Titrud farm there is a fine new house built. We cannot understand how people here can get along on so little land and put up such nice houses.

On the way up to Titrud we visited Mary Lie's home and Einar Lie who is her nephew. They showed me her picture. They claimed they still live in the old house. This afternoon Ole Lie, Einar's brother, called here. He is Mary's nephew. He remembered grandpa very well and also my father and uncle Henry. He invited us to come there; he is a very nice old man.

April 27. Today we visited Odd Ostmoe. We were invited there for dinner at 2pm. They have a nice home, but they told us it is very old.

His wife is from Romerike; they have no children. Odd is Ole Ostmoe's son, very quiet and reserved.

April 28. Today we visited Kolbjorn Ostmoe, son of Haakon, and were there for dinner. They live on the old Ostmoe farm. They have recently moved here and have built up everything new, so it is the most modern farm we have seen in Norway. Here in Solor most of the homes have electric lights.

April 29. Today we visited Amanda, Ole's daughter. She is married to Strand and lives close to her father's place. She has seven children, five girls and two boys. They bought this place 13 years ago and have a nice home according to Norwegian standards, radio, electric lights, etc.

April 30. This morning is bright and sunny. We are invited to Ole Lie, Mary Lie's nephew for coffee at 11 o'clock. We had a very fine lunch at Ole Lie. They had a big beautifully trimmed cake and many other cakes. They are Christian people and very interested and posted on church work. We enjoyed our visit very much. This afternoon we had a very fine dinner at Rolf Ostmoes, son of Ole Ostmoe. They have a very fine home. His wife comes from Austad, where Ole has his farm. She is a very fine woman. She sang and played for us.

May 1. We attended services in Hoff church this morning. This is Labor Day in Norway. After church we went to Ragnhilds where her brother Henrik and family and Kolbjorn were waiting for us. Henrik lives in Oslo and works in Hypotek Banker. He travels around and figures the value of forests. We will visit them later. Henrik has a fine Ford so he took us to George Ostmoes, Uncle Ole's old home where we were to have dinner. His wife is very able and seems to be a fine lady. Uncle Ole's widow is still alive, 75 years old.

Aunt Milla told me she had seen my great grandmother, my grandfather's mother. My grandfather was born on the Titrud farm. My father had a sister who died at a young age. Aunt Milla and Uncle Haakon cut grain together to earn a little money.

May 2. Otto Bjertnes called on us. He knew my father and mother and had worked together with my father. He is 69 years old and has been in Norway the last 20 years. He is a very interesting man and is well posted on American news. At 11:30am we bade Ragnhild and Oivind goodbye. Henrik and wife also came to see us off. We got a taxi to Arneberg and took a very interesting train trip to Elverum, an hour and a half ride. The farms in Norway are well kept, clean and the houses are nicely painted. Cousin Leif met us with both car and truck to take us to Haustad Farm where Uncle Per had his summer place. Uncle Per was a millionaire, owned two stores and carried on a big business. He lived in Elverum but had this as his summer home. This house is 30 years old but still a beautiful place. It lies on the edge of Glommen River and is an ideal home. Now Leif who was married last year runs it as a farm. Uncle Per's wife died long ago. He then remarried and is survived by his wife Mina. He died in 1921. Aunt Mina met us with a broad smile.

The month of May we spent visiting my relatives in Kappang. We met so many of them and they are flourishing. They have a large home and were able to accommodate all of us in a splendid way. We learned so much about my great grandparents and their children. My mother must have gone to America when she was about 20 years old. Yesterday we had snow and it got cold. The kids are learning to ski and enjoy taking many flops while trying to learn.

One thing we observed that is very interesting; the trend now is for families to preserve old things, family heirlooms, antiques, old furniture, old style clothes, the older the better, even recovering old customs, including language and names. On May 9 at 2:15pm we boarded a train for Trondheim. Arlene had a nerve removed from a tooth and she had a headache. We had a whole compartment to ourselves. We could see the homes built on the very edge of cliffs and up the mountainsides. Daddy thought it was too scary to enjoy. How can people live on such a small piece of land? Yet, they have big barns so they must have cattle, but what they have to feed them is difficult to see. We changed trains at 9:10pm and from there the snow became less and less as we descended. The grass is quite green and the trees are beginning to show life. We arrived in Trondheim at 11 o'clock and went to the Inner Mission Hotel where we got very fine rooms, very good beds and well furnished. I am sure it will cost plenty too.

May 10. Today we were permitted to enter the Dom-kirke. We spent over an hour in it, climbed the tower 172 steps. The church is a wonderful structure, very artistic with an awful lot of carvings in stone. Many of them are centuries old, even going back 1000 years. The large window is given by the women of Norway, costing $50,000. The big bell in the top of the tower is a meter in diameter.

May 11. We have been tramping all over town this morning. We saw the house where the Bishop lives. The next day we did not do much of anything. We are all tired so we are just taking it easy. May 13 we left early in the morning for Oslo by train. On May 24 we had to tend to business. This evening we went to Holmenkollen. The kids climbed the ski track. May 15 we went to church at Trinity Church and had a good dinner at a hotel. Then we went to the harbor to see the S. S. Oslofjord which had just docked a couple of hours before. After that we went to Frogner Park, a very beautiful place. In the evening the Sivesind sisters dropped in to visit.

May 16. After a lot of running around to offices taking care of our baggage, we finally slipped through customs safely. At 3 o'clock we were invited to Henrik Ostmoes for dinner and met more cousins: Odveig, Solveig, Ragnhild, Magne and wife, Astrid Dorum and her three children. Magne is in charge of a large silver fox farm, which has 250 small foxes.

May 17 is the Norwegian National Holiday and we are celebrating. We were on deck at 8:30am and placed ourselves on the top step of the steps leading up to the Royal Palace. We could see the whole parade as it came up Karl Johan Avenue. We had a good view of the Crown Prince and family. The King and Queen were absent. We saw the princesses Ragnhild and Astrid and Prince Harald. There must have been thousands in the parade, which seemed to take hours to pass. In the afternoon at 5pm we were invited to Astrid Ostmoe for lunch. Rolf, her only son, is studying to become a doctor. His father and grandfather were doctors.

May 19. This morning we left for Telemark, only three and a half hours from Oslo, and took a taxi to Rugtveits. Rugtveit was married to Ingeborg, daddy's sister. He was a teacher but now receives a pension from the

State. Ingeborg died in 1930 at the age of 48, leaving seven children. One can readily see that they have been brought up in a Christian home.

May 23. Today papa and I took the train to Bö to visit some of his friends and relatives. The children remained at Rugtveits. After arriving in Bö we went first to the cemetery where papa's parents are buried. There is a nice stone on their graves. The forget-me-nots were in full bloom between the graves. There is a very ancient stone church beside the new church. The inscription on Braaten's grave stone is: Folkvard Olsen Braaten, born 13-3-1850, died 28-2-1915. His wife's grave stone reads: Aslaug Braaten, born 5-7-1849, died 27-10-1908. Scripture passage: Philippians 3: 20.

After we left the cemetery we went to Halvor Nordbo. Both he and his wife were good friends of papa when he was a boy. They had a good time recalling memories of the old times. We were there for both dinner and coffee. The next day we visited Papa's teacher, Gjermund Oterholt.

May 22. We returned to Rugtveits last night and this morning we all went to Dalen by boat. Next we went to Skien to visit papa's oldest brother Hans and his wife Aase. They have five children. Hans has been rather unfortunate; he lost his farm and has gone from one place to another. We remained in Skien for two days; we lived at the hotel but ate at Hans's place. Hans works on the road as a mason. One day we walked up to the old Braaten farm where papa grew up. He says it is the same as when he was there thirty years ago.

June 8. Tomorrow we are to leave for Oslo which is the beginning of our return home to America and the end of our visit here in Norway. We regret that we have to leave now just as the summer begins. It is beautiful here now and we all feel comfortable. We are sitting here in Akerhaugen waiting for a train. We said goodbye to the Rugtveits and left for Oslo at 8am. We all had learned to know each other so it is with sadness that we part, realizing that we may never see each other again. We are now at the missionary home in Oslo. The city is filled with outsiders. We have our tickets and are ready for our journey home.

June 12. We boarded the train for Bergen and the next morning we got on the steamship S. S. Vega for New Castle. The trip was not so pleasant; we all got sea sick. It took us twenty hours to get to New Castle. From New Castle we took a train to London. We looked forward so much to seeing England, but alas we were greatly disappointed. All we saw from the train was one factory town after the other with clouds of smoke. The farms are old and dilapidated and the houses all look alike, so monotonous. None are beautiful. Well, we got to London and are staying at the National Hotel. We have two days to stay.

June 15. We went sightseeing all around the city. We saw the London Tower with all its jewels, St Paul's Cathedral, Big Ben, Queen Mary's Palace, Buckingham Palace where the King lives, the changing of the guards, Trafalgar Square, etc. The next day we took the train out to Beaconsfield where the Lilliput Gardens are. A miniature village is built there in a rich man's garden, so beautiful. We took a walk in the town to see the beautiful homes where the wealthy live in the summer time. The train ride took an hour each way so we did not manage more. We are good and tired, ready for dinner and sleep.

June 17. Finally, the day has arrived when we can actually start our journey to the U.S.A. We got to Southhampton at 10 o'clock ready to board the S. S. Washington. The train took us right to the docks. Now we are settled in our cabins, papa and Folkvard in one and the rest of us in the other. The cabins are nice and roomy but very plain. The dinner was good and the apple pie was a treat. And believe me, we did not forget the ice cream. Daddy thought we were hoggish to ask for both pie and ice cream, but we have it coming, so why not? The sea is marvelous and quiet as a lake. We certainly are fortunate and have much for which to be thankful with such wonderful care all along the way. I think of the words of the hymn, "God will take care of you!" The steamer chairs which we still have with us from Madagascar will come in handy. They are on deck now and we hope to make good use of them. God's promise for today: John 11: 27-29.

June 27. Here we are sitting in Penn Station in New York City waiting for a train to Chicago. Our voyage across the Atlantic was fine. There were many Jews on the boat. The last day was so foggy that we could only go at half speed and when we finally came within four miles of New York, we had to anchor for the night. That day we reached the docks at 2:30pm. It took us seven hours to land. It was tiresome to wait so long with baggage in hand. Rev. Pederson met us in his car and took us to Norway House. On Sunday we attended church service at the Plymouth Congregational Church, an old church Lincoln had attended here and we sat in a pew called Lincoln's pew. This church was built in 1860. In the afternoon we took a bus ride to 207th St. We rode down Broadway, along the Hudson River. We saw Grant's Tomb, Riverside Church, and other sights. We took the bus back. We also went to Radio City to see a play.

We are now waiting for a train. Oh, such a crowded city New York is. The streets are filled with cars, so it takes a long time to get anywhere. Fortunately we allowed plenty of time but it made me nervous. We got on the train safely and I was so glad to leave New York. We were in a sleeper car and were very comfortable. We arrived in Chicago at 7:30 the next morning. We had to get busy to board the next train to Minneapolis — get breakfast, clergy fares, tickets, check trunks, buy lunch, etc. The next train is to leave at 10:15am. We just made it in good time, so here we are to begin the last lap of our journey. It is hard to realize we will be in Minneapolis tonight. Won't we be happy?

We reached Minneapolis at 7:50pm the same day, nine and a half hours from Chicago. We were quite surprised to see so many there to meet us — Olga's and Augusta's families, Rev. Gronli, Sister Anna, Rev. Burgess, Rev. Schroeder, Arne and Roald Carslon. It was nice to be met by friends and relatives. We went with Olga and Augusta to their homes. Tomorrow afternoon we plan to move into our future home, Cottage No. 7 in St. Anthony Park, near Luther Seminary, in St. Paul.

1940. We are now in Cottage No. 7. We have enjoyed our furlough but now it is soon ended and we must start to get ready for our return to Madagascar. I have not taken the time to make entries into my diary during the short time we have been on furlough. Arlene was confirmed January 28 at the Sunday morning services. She was dressed in a gown with a spray of a red rose. She looked so nice. Rybergs and Nortons were there for the day.

February 1. I brought Agnes and Arlene to Canton, South Dakota, where they will make their home at Augustana Academy. I know they will be taken care of, but no one knows what it is like to say farewell to their children and to be separated for such a long time. May God bless them and keep them from all danger.

March 1. This last month has been a busy time for us. With house cleaning, washing of curtains, blankets, etc., shopping and parties, it seems to be getting too much at one time. Mrs. Burgess gave a nice party for me. Mrs. H. B. Kildahl gave a very fine lunch and also Mabel gave a party for some of us old timers, Anna Weeks, Cora, Selma, Ella and her daughter. Our last meals were at Lees, Blys, and Holm. Stolees also gave a fine dinner and we were invited. Mrs. Preus offered to take us to the station, which we were happy to accept. Our pieces of baggage were as filled and stuffed as could be. At the station many of our friends came to see us off. I will name them so I can remember them for their kindness: Nortons, Rybergs, Uncle Henry, Emma, Rev. Gronli, Rev. and Mrs. Langemo, Rev. and Mrs. Gornitzka, Mr. and Mrs. Dalland, Laura Eng, Nora Rosvold, Rev. Schroeder, Miss Nakling, Mrs. Vaageness and her two sons, Carl and Morris, Lyla and Palma Sivesind, Don Shore, and Edith.

Our train left at 8pm from the Great Northern Station on the Challenger. We had a nice trip to San Francisco that took two days and three nights. All in all it was rather monotonous. Crossing the Salt Lake Bridge was interesting to see. For miles there is nothing but sand. The trestle across the lakes is 15 miles long. We have good service on the train, breakfast 25 cents, lunch 30 cents, and dinner 35 cents, plus 10% tips. We arrived in San Francisco at 8:30am.

March 8. We took a taxi to Hotel Power where we got a comfortable room. That same morning we went to Montgomery Ward where we bought a stove, mattress, and two bikes for the boys. Mrs. Rateaver came to pick us up by car to take us for a ride around this beautiful and hilly city. Some of her children were with her, Demophile, Adelheit, and Claudia. We came back to the hotel at 6pm and invited them to have dinner with us. After supper they insisted that we should see Twin

Peaks. What a marvelous sight! The city of San Francisco, Oakland, Berkeley and other suburbs lie before us like a crazy quilt, all lit up. A wonderful sight.

March 11. This day we used to finish up our business affairs. The next day it was time for our departure. We arrived at the docks okay. Mrs. Rateaver, Mrs. Haferman, Rev. and Mrs. Gudmunsen came to see us off. It seemed like a dream that we should start off again on this long journey back to Madagascar for the third time. All our preparation and plans have been carried out so wonderfully. We are fully assured that the Lord is calling us out again. It has been more sad for us to leave the homeland this time. Many of those we know will have passed away during the next seven years. We had a strange feeling leaving the shores of America.

March 16. We had quite a rough sailing after leaving San Francisco. Our boat is the S. S. Cleveland, one of the President lines. The cabins are roomy, but our two cabins are the very last cabins in tourist class in the rear of the boat, so that when it is rough, we get the worst of it. Folkvard and I were quite miserable a couple of days, but today I feel well. I cannot brag about the food. The pie crusts are thick and heavy, their bread and buns are very poor. The food contains a lot of grease and gravies. The baked potatoes are like cold dumplings. An Indian lady from Rangoon is very interesting to talk to. She is a teacher and has been studying in the States. She has been teaching in a Baptist Mission College for sixteen years and speaks very good English. She always dresses in her Indian costume.

March 17. Palm Sunday. At 11am we had church service with papa leading it. At 4pm we landed in Honolulu. We went ashore and took a bus out to Waikiki, to the end of the line. We got off at the park and saw the birds at the zoo. Hawaii has a wonderful variety of plant life and Honolulu is a real flower garden wherever you go. At midnight we began sailing for Yokohama, Japan. March 22. Today is Good Friday. We have set our clocks back 30 minutes each day since we left the States and today we skip a day from Wednesday to Friday. We are having very fine weather so I am feeling pretty good. There will be two church services this afternoon. We don't know who is to lead them. The boys are having fun with the games. We all feel well. The bread even looks better now.

Easter Sunday. The sea is very rough today. The ship rolled and tipped so the dishes went flying off the tables. At 8am we received an SOS from a freighter that its pumps were not working. We were 157 miles away. We did not reach it until 8pm. We stayed there until 6:30 the next morning when we were finally notified that they got the pumps working again. At 11am we had church services with Rev Ylvisaker officiating. Next Sunday will be papa's turn again.

March 29. We arrived at Yokohama 11:50am yesterday. We had dinner and got off about 2pm. We hired a taxi for 4 yen; the exchange is 4 yen to the dollar, but on the boat they exchange it 6 yen for the dollar. We rode all around the city, saw the residential district, a Buddhist temple, the European and Japanese shopping district, Chinatown, and had tea at a Japanese restaurant. We went to a native shopping area where the shops look much like the 10 cent stores in America. Cheap stuff. Of course, there are expensive stores too. On our way back to the boat we bought several souvenirs right on the dock. Both papa and I got Japanese kimonos. I paid 10 yen and papa 15.

The people here are well dressed, the men wearing suits and overcoats and the women the traditional Japanese costume. The young girls and women are rather pretty but the men look very homely to us, with big jaws and teeth and wide flat faces. The Buddhist temple was not a bit attractive and the seats were uncomfortable. Several man-size statues were lined up in front of the temple. We had to cover up our shoes with a sort of sock and the boys had to remove theirs.

Many of the passengers, in fact, most of them, bought tickets to go across land to Kobe via Tokyo. After a lot of deliberation we decided not to go. When they got to the Imperial Hotel in Tokyo to investigate about trains, they found no accommodations at hotels nor reservations on trains, so they all came back very disappointed. But Lyla, the Indian woman and another woman did not return. We are to arrive in Kobe this evening, 8pm.

March 30. This morning Lyla, Miss Santay, the boys and I hired a taxi and went sightseeing for two hours. We saw two shrines and one huge Buddha. People came and went continually, each one throwing a coin into a large container, bowing and clapping their hands and repeating their prayers. The shopping district is very crowded. We spent ten dollars in Japan. Enough!

March 31. Papa led the church service this morning. We landed in Manila April 4. We had a very fine sea from Kobe. Today is very hot in Manila. We had to get our passports visaed for Saigon, India, Reunion and a landing visa for Tamatave. Were we ever roasted by the time we got our baggage through the customs. We got a room at the Marco Polo Hotel. We have to pay 12.50 pesos per room, about $6.50 per day. If we take our meals here it will be $11.50 per day. That is high so we are fortunate that we do not have to stay here long. We are permitted to take our meals on the Cleveland as long as it is in port.

April 8. We boarded Boissevain at 4pm yesterday. Papa brought the heavy baggage on the day before. On Saturday afternoon we went to the Lyric to see Swanee River, a play about Stephen Foster, the writer of many Black songs, like Old Black Joe, Swanee River, etc. It was nice and cool in there, so it was a treat for us, since it has been very hot in Manila. The streets are very crowded with cars, rickshas and people. Taxis are very reasonable but everything else is high in price. Milk is 25 cents a quart. Food is twice as high as in America. Everything in the stores is imported from the U. S. or Japan.

This boat is the finest we have ever been on. It was built in 1937 so it has been on sea only two years. Everything is modern, roomy, and luxurious. Our cabins are very fine. We have free steamer chairs, electric irons, swimming pool and all kinds of games. It is too warm in our cabins, but nice and cool on deck and in sitting rooms.

April 10. We arrived in Saigon yesterday at 3:30pm, a port in French Indo-China. We together with Lyla Sivesind took a rickshaw uptown and went to some of the shops. Saigon is a beautiful town, big houses with verandas. They are all whitewashed in cream lime so they look nice and clean. The next morning we hired a taxi for three piasters per hour.

We visited a pagoda where the Chinese worship. We were permitted to go in and see their altars and way of worship. They knelt and bowed and repeated their prayers. There were many beautiful gold vases, swords and other ornaments. I bought only two lace handkerchiefs and a center piece for the dinner table. We stayed in Saigon from Wednesday afternoon until Thursday afternoon. The large boats must wait for the tide to rise. We also saw a beautiful park which is really artistic. A large zoo is connected with it, with both lions and tigers.

While in Saigon we learned about Germany invading and occupying Denmark and Norway. What a shock! What next? On April 13 we arrived in Bangkok at 6:30am. It is quite warm and sultry here. Bangkok is way up the river 35 miles. It takes about four hours in a launch to get there. Those who wish to go there must take the cholera serum, so we are staying on board. Neither are the Ylvisakers and Sivesind. We will be here for three days. There is a nice breeze, however, so it is not so bad. A few of the passengers have a stomach ache, so we had better be careful what we eat. Carl has caught a cold. A couple of peddlers are on board with jewelry items, but I am afraid they may not be genuine. Well, I dickered with one peddler until I finally bought five pins and one belt buckle for $5.00. It is typical Bangkok work so I felt I wanted it. Yesterday a few of us went with a couple of officers in their launch to an island. There was an ancient summer resort for the Siamese king. It was a beautiful place once upon a time. Siam changed government a year ago and is called Thailand now. Their king is still a small boy, attending school in England.

The war news is getting more and more dreadful. Germany is sending troops to Norway and so is Britain. It looks like Norway might become a real battlefield. What a change from what it was two years ago when we were there.

April 17. We just arrived in Singapore at 10:30am outside the harbor. There are a lot of small islands. We have gone through mine fields for a whole day and night. I was told that the hills are heavily armed against invasion. We are waiting for inspection. Singapore is a British Protectorate. We went out for a ride to the Botanical Gardens. Such a beautiful garden with the most luxurious foliage and flowers I have ever seen. We fed the monkeys bananas as they came running down from the trees from every direction. For the first time I saw how the mother monkey carries her young. We also visited a Buddhist and a Moslem temple so we had to take off our shoes. Several men were there to worship. No women were allowed in the temples. We also visited a wealthy Chinese home. The owner built it purposely for visitors, so our driver told us. It was luxurious, to say the least. He had a large number of ornaments made from precious stones. Around the courtyard he had China built in miniature. Passages were built in and out from one room to another. It looked like solid worn down rocks but actually it was all made of cement. His wife and daughter sat there, but they were dressed as simple as could be. The mother had packed cards in her hand.

April 19. We arrived in Batavia, Dutch West Indies, at noon today. Lyla, the boys and I went for a long walk. Batavia is very low above sea level. There are canals built criss-cross throughout the city for navigation. They say we will have four days here, so today we went sightseeing. We hired a taxi to take us around to see the Botanical Gardens. First we went to the Aquarium only to find it closed. Then we stopped at an old Portuguese Church built in 1762. There was no altar but the pulpit was up front in the center. Then we visited an interesting museum and saw all kinds of ancient things from the different islands. Then we drove through the old town and the new to the Botanical Gardens. These are the most famous gardens in the world. Along most of the way were homes and stores, and here and there were beautiful homes with lovely lawns and gardens, with a rich variety of trees and bushes. And the houses are artistically built and colored. The Botanical Gardens have a rich variety of trees from other tropical countries. I have never seen such large trees. The stone walks are interesting to see but not to walk on. They are winding and laid over little hills and across bridges. Many of the large trees were covered with parasites of different kinds. We saw the garden orchids. The governor's palace is next to the garden, and what a palace it is. By this time we were tired and hungry so we went to the Keyser Hotel for lunch, but they served a big dinner, much too big for us.

And much too expensive. We rested a bit and then went to the "Pasar" market where we got some mangosteen, and they were so good. They are about the size of an apple, with a thick layer of red meat and inside some white layers of fruit. We then decided to return to Batavia and see some more of the town. We stopped to see Wilhelmina's Park, the old fort and the cathedral. The citadel at the old fort was built in 1760. The rice fields were wonderful.

April 21. Sunday morning, we are counting the days until we get to Tamatave, Madagascar. On Monday we took a taxi again to the museum. We bought some bookends.

April 30. We arrived in Mauritius this morning. We went ashore on the ship's launch. We have had quite a bit of company, with a Swedish couple from Los Angeles by name of Holm. They asked us to go with them for a ride. We drove a good forty miles, first again to the Botanical Gardens and then to the beach. This port, Port Louis, is a beautiful place with high mountains in the background. Our 80 mile ride was a grand treat after so many days on the ocean.

May 2. We hope to reach Tamatave today. We have had very fine sailing ever since we left Yokohama. I am a very poor sailor, and even at that I have not missed a meal. I have gone to the table every time except for the first breakfast. The boys have had a wonderful time playing ping pong and swimming. We have had a very generous menu but even so I am getting tired of it. We were in Reunion yesterday but we did not step off because we had some packing to do. When we arrived in Tamatave, we were anxious to learn what accommodations we could get to Fort Dauphin. We got hold of Ducomen first of all, and found out that the Le Petit Norwegian was in harbor, sailing for Fort Dauphin, so we made arrangements to take it. But we had a big job to get all of our baggage off this boat and on to another one. We made it hurriedly through customs. We had to pay 800 francs on two bikes, mattresses, stove, and the Chinese chest. Then we boarded the little coast steamer. Papa decided to go to Tananarive to buy a car. We sailed at 9:30pm for Vatomandry.

The trip was uneventful. The little boat went from port to port, unloading and loading freight, first to Manoro, then to Mananjary. It was so slow that I wished we would have gone overland with Papa.

May 9. Now we are nearing Fort Dauphin, our final destination. A new white cement landmark has been erected since we left. There are quite a few people standing on the quad, missionaries and children from the school. We waved to each other. It gave me a thrill and a lump in my throat. I did not expect that papa would be among them to greet us. The sea was rough. The little boat we were supposed to get in to take us to land was jumping up and down, making me scared. When I saw papa there, he told me that missionary Carlson had died, so he bought his car. It certainly was unexpected sad news. Carlson died from typhoid just three weeks before. We also got news that we had been placed in Manafiafy, a little town on the coast.

May 22. We left for Manafiafy, having spent two weeks in Fort Dauphin. It is different for us to have such a short drive to our station, only 53 kilometers or 32 miles. On June 2 we celebrated our 18th anniversary. I made a cake and we invited Miss Olson, Miss Stevenson, and Mrs. Martin to join us. We worked to get ourselves settled in our new home, all the curtains hung, everything scrubbed clean, and got the garden well on its way. There are all kinds of trees in the garden, orange, lemon, papaya, coconut, banana, coeur de boeuf, zaty, pineapple, bamboo, rose bushes, grape vines, etc. We hope we will have plenty of fruits some day.

Today we got news that Italy has declared war on England and France. Oh, what a world we are living in. One third of France is already occupied by Germany, and is already asking for peace terms. On June 29 France quit fighting and signed an armistice in which Paris is turned over to the enemy. We got a letter from Torvik saying that Germany is in control of all of France.

July 4. We celebrated this holiday by having supper for all the missionaries, Misses Olson, Stevenson, Sivesind and Madame Martin. I made a white cake with an American flag in the middle.

July 14 is the French national holiday, so we hoisted the French flag and weighed ourselves. It is peaceful here but not so in many parts of the world.

September 5. We returned yesterday from Fort Dauphin, after having brought Folkvard and Carl back to school. We all had a good time during their vacation. Kittel and family spent nine days here. Misses Rorstad, Nybroten and Rindal also visited Manafiafy. We celebrated Anna's birthday with a surprise party. Roald, Arndt and Olaf also biked out for a couple of days. We have had no mail since the middle of August. We can still get the necessary things in Fort Dauphin except flour and soap. Fortunately we have some on hand.

September 11. It's papa's birthday, but no cake. We had a triple birthday cake before the boys went back to school. Folkvard had one candle for 13 years. I had 4 for 46 and papa 5 for 52. How times does fly.

October 7. We attended the annual conference of our district. Torvik met us in Bakika with his Ford, as the ferry that takes us across the river was washed away in a storm. He also met Stolee in Ampasimena. By that time the car was having trouble so it could not make the hills. So the Stolees, Misses Sivesind, Olson, and Stevenson and ourselves had to return by "fillanzana."[3] I enjoyed it, for a change. This way I could relax except when the carriers went too fast. And fast they went the last half day. There are five rivers to cross between here and Manantenina. The road follows the sea coast the whole way. One can see the ocean from a distance most of the way.

We had a very pleasant time with our co-workers and the meeting was very successful. The talks and discussions were well prepared. It was thrilling to see Manantenina again. But there was one thing that made my heart very sad and that was to see Randria. He was a faithful and honest worker in Bekily, so we learned to love and respect him. But he was struck down with paralysis that left his whole right side helpless. He then went home to his father with his family and his herd of oxen. The father is an old heathen and he took possession of Randria's cattle and starved out the poor wife and child. Randria is looked upon as an idiot possessed by an evil spirit. Both of us visited him and he seemed normal to talk to. What a calamity, to see what he has to go through.

How about our work here in Manafiafy? To us as new beginners it

---

[3] Filanzana is Malagasy for palanquin.

looks very discouraging. There are no congregations to speak of in this area. Our house is so far away from the people that they do not come here. It looks like it will be difficult to do any effective work here. Many have been baptized here, but where are they now?

Papa is putting a new roof on the church here. Right now he is getting his wind charger. We have had no letters from America since the middle of July. How we long to hear from our dear girls. My heart is aching!

November 18. The war is raging. Italy and Greece are fighting. Germany has invaded Romania. The American fleet is ready to defend her islands. Yesterday Papa and I went bathing way over in the second bay from here, a swell place to bathe.

November 25. We finally received some mail. It was a real whiff from home to get some papers, even though they were six to seven months old. Yet, no letters from Agnes or Arlene. But it stated in the Canton paper that Arlene was to play in the graduation exercises.

December 6. What a joy! We got a letter from Arlene, written May 5 but mailed in Canton May 27.

December 30. Christmas is past. Papa and I attended the children's Christmas program in Fort Dauphin and took the boys back to the station. It seems good to be back together again. But there are not many things for them to do. We had some excitement here in town some weeks ago. The pastor's house was in full blaze at 2 o'clock past midnight. Miss Stevenson hollered and pounded on the door to wake us up. What a shock when we did wake up!

January 3. Carl's birthday! We made a cake and had it for our coffee. After we had cleared the table the four ladies here at the station stepped over with a fine chocolate cake.

January 12. Our first Sunday on Lebanon. We left the station on the 7th. We are having lovely weather. Everybody is well and happy to be together. We are having Mr and Mrs. Bjelde over for supper tonight. This month the missionary conference met. Papa is to peach the sermon. We had Bible lectures every forenoon. Both Carl and I have come down with a real attack of fever and we both have received hypos.

February 19. This is my first day up after my second attack of fever here on Lebanon. I must need to be more regular in taking quinine.

Because of the war the missionaries who are due to return home on furlough have no chance of leaving the island. The war clouds are gathering everywhere. The Germans are even preparing to attack England. By the time I got over my fever attacks, Folkvard came along with some unexpected trouble. He stepped on a sea urchin and it left some needles in his toe. We could not see any, so we did not take him to a doctor. It became very painful and after a week, it still remained swollen. We then took him to a doctor, and he found three needles in his toe. He had to operate. A big puss bag formed, so the doctor had to lance it. We hope now for a speedy recovery. The sea urchin is a round animal the size of an egg and covered with long needles about two inches long. Those are their protection. They inject them into the flesh and leave them there. They are poisonous but not deadly. School began but Folkvard could not go.

March 14. We are back at the station. There had been no heavy rains, so the road was good. It had also been repaired. We found everything as we had left it.

March 17. Last night a storm came up. It started to rain the night before with a strong wind. It continued to rain off and on until Sunday night when the wind increased to a gale that sounded like a hurricane was coming. After a while I was awakened by a rattling and pounding on the front corner of the house. I went out to look and saw that the roof was coming off. I got nervous about this. Papa slept and never heard a thing, so I called him. He got up and saw that this was serious. So he ran to the garage and got some ropes to tie down the old roof. When he got back with the ropes, which was only a few minutes, the roof of one third of the house and veranda was ripped off and thrown way over the house and into the garden. The rest of the veranda roof was hanging in the air, as the veranda posts had ripped out too. If this could not be tied down, the whole roof would fly off. So papa got out there in the terrible rain and wind on the upstairs veranda with the ropes. The roof pounded up and down so I was afraid that it might fall on him. It was a risky job, but he finally succeeded. The wind was furious, as if it was ready to destroy everything. Even the house shook. We had to move out of one half of the house, which took us until 3 o'clock in the morning. An enormous damage was done throughout the island. Our house looks terrible, but we have to say as Pollyanna said when something went wrong, "I'm glad it did not go worse." We just got a letter from Fort Dauphin and were glad to hear the boys are safe. Half of the roof on the seminary director's house where Mrs. Carlson and children live was torn off. Three of our churches fell flat. The mission will suffer a big loss on buildings.

Aptril 24. A week ago yesterday papa and I went to Fort Dauphin with a sick girl from our school. That night I had an attack of fever; I froze and perspired all night. We went back to the station the next day and I was running a temperature. I had to go to bed and three more days of continual fever. I took three quinines the first day and three a day for five days. After I was through with this treatment, I was as weak as a new born calf. I am recovering a little day by day.

The war is still going on. Greece has surrendered to the Germans and also Yugoslavia. The war is going on in North Africa and Lybia. There has been a big battle in Crete for two weeks. The British had to surrender there too, with heavy losses on both sides. There is not a wall remaining of the beautiful Capitol of Crete.

July 24. The childrens' vacation began July 18. Papa and I and Miss Stevenson went to Fort Dauphin to fetch the boys. The war is still raging. Germany has entered Russia, and they have already fought for five weeks. England is bombing western Germany all she can. Now Japan is attacking Indo-China and Singapore. Fighting is going on near Leningrad; England is bombing Berlin. We listen to the news on radio every day.

We just finished our Annual District Conference here in Manafiafy. Mr. and Mrs. Torvik, Mr. and Mrs. Stolee, and Sister Mette came. The attendance was good and so was the program. We sincerely hope that those who attended experienced the power of the Word in their hearts that will change them and make them more earnest and sincere in serving the living God.

The German invasion of Russia seems to be progressing for them. We hear of fierce fighting towards Moscow and in the Ukraine. Leningrad has not yet fallen. This is the 19th week since Germany declared war on Russia. We are both well and so are the boys. Bjeldes, Andersons, Carlsons, and Miss Olson left on an American boat October 19.

December 4. Our Six Months' Meeting began today. Yesterday was the day for preparation. Everybody was washing up and getting ready while those from the country were arriving. But what a preparation. A fire had broken out and every man was called out to fight. A few of the school girls had built a fire to cook rice down by the river. It was a windy day and sparks were blown into the dry grass. Before they knew it, the fire was roaring and it continued on in the big forest of travelers palms. It began at 11 o'clock in the morning and was not put out until evening. The people became very exhausted. But that was not enough. During the night it flared up again and the men were called out. But in spite of all this, we began the meeting the next morning. This noon the fire began again, and word came that all the men must go. But then they saw the fire was going out again, so now we hope we shall not have any more disturbances. A week ago the lightning struck the tower of the church. It tore off the cross and ripped off the shingles and boards of the wall.

The war is still raging in Russia. The Germans are still pressing towards Moscow, but have not conquered Leningrad or Sebastapol. Bitter fighting around Kharkov, Ukraine. War is threatening to start in the Pacific. There are said to be negotiations between the United States and Japan. Japan wants the Burma road closed.

On December 8 Japan attacked the United States of America. They bombed the Philippine Islands, Hawaii, Singapore, landed troops in Malaysia in two different places, bombed Guam, other islands and Hong Kong. America lost 35 planes. England lost two of her finest battleships which had been sent to protect Malaysia. A U.S. minesweeper was sunk. Two thousand men on board were saved by a destroyer. Japan made these surprise attacks without declaring war. The next day the United States and Great Britain declared war on Japan. Other countries followed: Costa Rica, Venezuela, Columbia, China, Australia, and New Zealand. The following countries declared war on the United States and Great

Britain: Japan, Germany, and Italy. A big Japanese battleship of 29,000 tons was sunk by the United States. Guam was invaded by Japan and Manila was bombed constantly, especially the naval base. Troops also landed in the Philippines. The Russians are driving the German armies back in several places. Winter has set in so the enemy has given up trying to take Moscow for the time being. In southern Ukraine the Germans are being forced to retreat.

December 24. Folkvard and Carl came here on Monday for Christmas. They rode their bicycles and it took them four hours. We had a nice Christmas together as a family. The children's program in church on Christmas eve was unusual. After we got home we lit our tree and Carl distributed the gifts. On Christmas Day we were invited to Sivesind and Stevenson for dinner and on the second day of Christmas they came to our house. We heard rumors that there was famine in Fort Dauphin, so we were not so anxious to go to Lebanon this year. We left for Lebanon nonetheless on the 6th of January and today I can say we are settled. Rabia is our house boy and doing fine. Gilbert is our cook but I am not so sure how long he will last. I am afraid his dishonesty will deprive him of a lasting job here.

Feb. 1. Our Mission Conference begins on Sunday. Services will be conducted this afternoon by Rev. Munson. Everybody in the Mission colony is well. The Conference met at the M. C. Home and Lebanon alternatively. We were moved to Behara. So last week papa and I went to Manafiafy to pick up all our goods. Today some of the missionary children are being confirmed: Folkvard, Olaf, Erling Stolee, and Gudrun Hofstad. Uncle Kittel is the presiding pastor.

March 18. We left for Behara. Our car was loaded to the top — stove, radio, two hens, a kitten and hundreds of other articles. We could not cross the river so all of our stuff had to be carried across by hand. We were very fortunate to get our baggage loaded in Lokhat's truck. It is getting very difficult now because of the shortage of gas.

March 21. We are now pretty well settled in Behara and feel at home. The house is pretty well furnished so we can make it home-like. Solomona is our cook and Gustave is our house boy.

May 7. The British have invaded Madagascar and the French are trying to resist. While we were listening to the news last night a telegram came from Cartford telling us that we need to meet the four Braaten boys and Norli's boys at Amboasary. The government is taking over the M. C. Home to use as a hospital, so the building had to be evacuated at once. Papa met them this forenoon. It was fun to see them come. We can hardly realize the seriousness of this. We sincerely hope that some agreement can be reached soon so that people here do not see the ravages of war. They are recruiting soldiers in Fort Dauphin and have set up a camp on the hill where the water tanks are that we see from the back porch of the home. The M. C. Home is ready now to take in patients. We hope that will not be needed. Olaf and Arndt were with us for only one week when Kittel and Anna came from Tananarive to fetch them.

June 2. Today is our 20th anniversary. The boys and I have made a lemon pie and cake and Folkie made candy. We invited Pastor Gilbert and wife and Candidate Marjoela and wife for tea this afternoon.

June 23. Folkvard and Carl went back to school riding their bikes. We have had a good time together. They made a trip by bike to Ambovombe last week to visit the Hofstads, who have three daughters, Gudrun, Louise, and Miriam. Schools are permitted to function again in Fort Dauphin after they have evacuated the M. C. Home. We got a telegram saying that the boys arrived at noon. That means it took them only four hours to peddle their bikes from Behara to Fort Dauphin, about 50 miles. The girls at school brought us a little pup as a gift. Papa wants to call him "Bakshish," not only because he is a gift but also he is a great beggar. In Arabic Bakshish is a word that beggars use in crying out for a gift.

August 15. There is a Fare here in Behara today and tomorrow. We strolled over for a while to see what's there. Here on the island everything is quiet now, no fighting, and there is no famine. But the natives are very anxious about what to wear, because no cloth can be had at any price. Those who like to dress up have clothes, but those who have one set of garments find that they are getting ragged and some are even naked.

August 19. For days Mother's diary summarizes the daily news about the war, its progress and regress, in all parts of the world where World War II was going on between the Allies and the Axis in Europe, Africa, and Asia. In August and September the war is beginning to turn in favor of the Allies. Russia is beating back the Germans. The combined forces of Great Britain, the United States, and the Free French are winning in North Africa, Italy, and France. Closer to home the British made some landings in Majunga, Nossi Bé and Morondava in the northern part of the island. They are meeting very little resistance. They are heading toward Tananarive, the capitol city. We hear that the city has been declared an open city, to spare it from war damage. There are rumors that the natives may rise up in revolt against the upper class. So people do not like to leave their homes in such uncertainty for any length of time. The roads are cut up and the canoes are hid in the woods so neither ox carts nor cars can go anywhere.

The British troops marched into Tananarive on September 23. All is quiet with no French army resistance. We happen to be well except for some fever aches in our bodies. The American school is functioning as usual. A British cruiser entered the harbor in Fort Dauphin. An envoy came ashore with the result that the French army capitulated on the spot, to avoid any bloodshed.[4]

November 19-22. Meanwhile with all the excitement about the news of the war turning in favor of the Allies everywhere, East and West, on the Atlantic and Pacific Oceans, the work of the Mission continued slowly and steadily. We held another Annual Conference that was well attended.

The British have taken over all government affairs in Madagascar. There was some stubborn resistance for a while before the French completely gave up. The Governor must be hiding somewhere because we do not hear any more of him. All the roads are open again and an allotment

---

[4] Mother did not know when she wrote about this event in her diary that Tack (Folkvard) and I were hiding in the bushes a few feet from where the envoy consisting of about twenty well-armed marines were marching up the hill to the Fort where the French army was expected to resist. But not a shot was fired. The French raised a white flag of surrender. It was an exciting and unforgettable experience for us to get a taste of World War II up close.

of mail came though last Saturday. For months we received no mail. When it finally came we got 8 letters from Arlene and a letter from Olga.

Christmas is approaching so fast. The boys will have to spend Christmas at the M. C. Home this year because we have no way of getting them here due to the lack of gas to run our car. So we had a quiet Christmas with Miss Henum as our guest. I finally got up enough ambition to trim our house and put up a nice tree. I got some flour from Anna so I could make a "*jule-kake*," a real treat for us.

December 31. We left for Fort Dauphin when papa fixed his tire after having worked on it for three days. All the missionaries have been able to come except three families. Obviously, no gas. Everyone seems to be well in our colony. Since this year I did not bring our cook and houseboy, I am quite busy doing the housekeeping.

March 10, 1943. The first ones left for their stations today. We waited until Sunday because we wanted to attend Marjoela's ordination. He worked in Sampona but will now be placed in Ranomafana with Ingara Nakling. Misses Dahl and Haugen left for Tananarive a month ago. Miss Dahl has inoperable cancer and is failing very rapidly, so it is only a question of time. Miss Haugen writes that she is very patient in her suffering and is longing to go home to be with her Savior. To hear the Word of God is her only request. In her telegram she quotes, Job 19, 25-27. "*For I know that my Redeemer lives, and at last he will stand upon the earth, and after my skin has been thus destroyed, then without my flesh I shall see God, whom I shall see on my side, and my eyes shall behold, and not another. My heart faints within me!*"

We have had a very peaceful vacation. The Conference was short and quiet. There were problems as usual but they were solved wisely. We are feeling the lack of missionaries, so the work will be heavier for the few who must fill the vacancies besides their own station. We are not suffering for any want yet. What we do not have in our storeroom, we simply have to do without. Sugar, kerosene, gas, flour, spices, soap, cloth, thread and other things are not for sale anymore. The same goes for any kind of school materials. We have on hand some of all these things, but soon we will be short of some of them.

March 18. Miss Dahl died last evening at 8 o'clock in Tananarive. Her body will be brought to Fort Dauphin to be buried in the mission cemetery.

May 18. Much has happened since last I wrote. Papa and I made a trip to Sampona where we had our Annual Conference. It was an interesting trip because it was the first time I went out to the outlying district since I came to Behara. Here is where I saw the Catechist's wife go out behind some bushes to deliver her own baby like an animal does when it is giving birth. After a few minutes she came along to go into her hut as if nothing had happened, nice and slender.

People are busy planting sweet potatoes and watching their rice fields ripen. If they do not guard their fields, the birds will strip them in a few hours. We are getting string beans for a change, but ever since we came back from Lebanon, we have not been able to buy a sprig of any green vegetable.

August 19. Folkvard and Carl left for school today. We learned that a commercial truck was ready to go to Fort Dauphin, so the boys got ready in a hurry and left at 2:30pm. We have enjoyed their stay here immensely. They went crocodile hunting with Gilbert Cabiro and stayed out two nights.

September 8. We had our Annual Conference in Antanimora this year. Hofstads were the hosts; we had a good meeting. The weather was ideal with beautiful moonlit nights. The bad news is that the famine is serious here and will be a knockout blow to thousands of people in Androy. The rice house for the school girls was robbed of a couple of sacks of rice. The thieves had left six sacks in the bushes hoping to fetch them later, but some children discovered them.

We just received authorization to buy 13 kilos of flour. We have not had wheat flour for a year and a half. We have got along fine with the substitutes we have made ourselves from rice, manioc, and ampemba. Was it ever a treat to get wheat bread again. It is very hot here in Behara, over 100 degrees in the shade. We are having an unusual drought. All the rivers are dried up, even the Mandrare. People born here say they cannot remember anything like the severe famine we are having this year. Papa bought rice, manioc, beans and corn, so we have plenty on hand to feed our workers and the school children.

Thanksgiving Day! No big dinner today! We are too busy to work in the kitchen. Today we are holding our last meeting and lesson this year in the Ladies Aid. We have been studying the Gospel of John and will finish it today. I have been forced to study quite a bit for these lessons. It has done a lot of good and I believe I have learned a lot of the Malagasy language too. I only wish the women would have done some studying as well.

After the long drought it began to rain today and were we happy. The smell of the rain and the pitter patter on the roof were a special treat. Papa put out all the pails he could find to catch the precious fresh water. Tomorrow I can wash my hair in soft water. The heat has been terribly intense and the air is full of dust and smoke. The cattle are dying by the thousands and there is hardly any food for the people, and what food is available is very expensive. We still have food for our workers and school children. In the last mail we got letters from Agnes and Arlene.

December 29. We left for Lebanon. We had the car on the other side of the river in case the river was too high to cross. So we crossed over the river by palanquin, but the water was so high that the water came up to my seat and got me all wet. I had to undress to dry out my clothes before we could start out again. We had a cage with 20 chickens on top of the car. We had the cat along with us but we left our dog Bakshish with Amosa. Solomona, our cook, and Robson, our houseboy and two other servants went before us, so we have good help this year.

February 13, 1944. Carl was confirmed this Sunday. Paul Norlie, Frederick Hallanger, Leif Solee, and Louise Hofstad were his classmates. Rev. Stolee presided at the service. Uncles, Cartfords, and Miss Nybroten are leaving on the Nidaros today. It is raining so hard that I am afraid the folks will get soaked getting on board.

March 21. We arrived in Behara today. We had a fine vacation after I was over with all my fever and treatment. The boys went back to school and the M. C. Home after supper. On our way to Behara we arrived at the river Menanara. It looked like it was passable, so we drove in and there we sat. The back wheels were digging in deeper and deeper into the sand until the water flowed into the car. Papa's books, our safe full of paper money and a flour sack got all wet. We had to unload and carry everything across the river by hand. And we made it safely.

Easter Sunday. Papa is making a tour through the southern part of the district, Ampasipolaka, Sampona, etc. It still continues to be hot and dry. The famine is increasing and an epidemic of typhoid has broken out. The little girl of our catechist, Jaona Tsangambelo, died from typhoid and now he has the fever too. Also many are dying from stomach troubles.

May 10, We received a telegram stating that Hortense Quanbeck died today at noon of yellow fever. What a shock! We had not heard anything of her illness.

May 25. Papa was given Tsivory too to take care of this year, so we left Behara this morning at 8am and arrived here in Tsivory early afternoon. It was hard getting across the river Mandrare and much of the road is stony, since the dirt has been washed away. What a difference this place is from Behara. Here the trees and the grass are flourishing and the roses are in full bloom. This looks like a paradise to us compared to Behara. We hear that Arndt and Olaf have left Tamatave but the rest are still awaiting to leave. Cartfords and Miss Nybroten are in South Africa. Arlene just graduated from Augustana Academy and Agnes finished her second year of college at Augustana in Sioux Falls.

July 5. We left Tsivory this morning at 11am for Amboamangy about 50 kilometers and arrived at 1 o'clock. Papa left the next morning by palanquin to Ranobe which took about six hours. I stayed alone all day and night. The church attendance in this village is very poor. It was a full moon so I did not mind being alone. What a gorgeous sunset. I sat in the car and watched the moon rise. On July 7 we returned to Behara and found everything okay. We were gone exactly six weeks. Our cat was found dead but Bakshish was fine and fat.

August 15. The boys came out here by Transsud to Amboasary and papa met them in the car. On Saturday we all drove to Sampona for the Six Months Meeting, stayed over night and returned Sunday afternoon.

Sampona is about five miles from the ocean. It lies high so one can see the ocean on two sides. The air is fine and there are no mosquitoes. Even though the town is so close to the ocean it is very dry in that district so they are getting no crops this year. Water must be carried long distances. We just heard from Kittels that they are leaving Madagascar now. Last Sunday we all drove to Amboasary for services.

September 5 is Folkvard's birthday. We had a good cake for him when he was here. They left for school on September 3. We got a letter from Arlene.

It is over a month since I wrote. Papa has been in Tsivory three weeks and will be gone two more weeks, so I am all alone. Time flies fast; I am busy all day with cooking, milk chores, etc., so I have no time to be lonesome. Just received three tons of corn and manioc. So now I can have the job of dishing it out again in kilos and cups. Kittel and family arrived in the States in October, seven months after they left.

December 2. Folkvard, Carl, Erling, Leif, and Cubby stayed over night last Saturday. It was fun to have them. On December 27 we left for Fort Dauphin after having spent Christmas here. Yet it is good to get to Lebanon to be with the boys and get together with friends. Yet, I suffered from fever all vacation. The week before Easter when we were supposed to return to Behara, I got a bad attack with 101 to 102 degrees temperature for three days. Miss Haugen came to nurse me. It was interesting to see how a nurse takes care of a fever patient. After five days of quinacrine and two days of quinine, I was as weak as a new born calf. Easter came on April 1, so we did not get to Behara for Easter this year. When we arrived here by the river, the water was so high we had to unload the car and carry everything up to the station. Then papa took the car and drove across. Some rocks rolled over and threw the car off the stone bridge, so one side of the car fell into the water. 15,000 francs got soaked so we had the same old dirty job we had last year, to separate all of them to dry.

We received the shocking news over the radio that President Roosevelt died yesterday afternoon. It seems that he would be needed now more than any other man in the whole world. There is no one to fill his place.

May 5. It was announced tonight that the German High Command has unconditionally surrendered. The war in Europe is over and the Nazi enemy is conquered. What a joyful news for the world, except for Germany and Japan. We had a very impressive church service this morning. Papa preached on II Samuel 1: 27: "How the mighty have fallen, and the weapons of war perished." A very fitting text for the occasion. The Primary School sang. We hope to hear this evening that Norway is also liberated.

July 9, 1946. Papa and I just returned this noon after a trip to Ampasipolaka, Sampona, Berenty, and Amboasary, the most important of our out-stations. It seems to us that more could be done if the catechists were more zealous. We got letters from Agnes and Arlene written months ago. We are waiting for more recent news from them.

August 12. The boys came here for vacation July 24. Knut Skarpaas is visiting us and the boys are having a good time.

August 24. Here we find ourselves in the midst of packing again. We are to move to Bekily to replace Hallangers. We have been here in Behara three and a half years. The boys returned to school and we just arrived in Bekily. We had a nice trip. Today is Sunday and we attended services in the new church. Pastor Johnson preached an impressive sermon. It was interesting to meet some of the faithful ones that we remember from our time here before. It seems strange that we should be returning to Bekily. We have a lot of house cleaning to do. Everything needs a good scrubbing.

Another week has passed. I am all in today, after supervising, scrubbing, putting up the drapes, the same ones I made for this house fifteen years ago.

The boys came out to Bekily to spend Christmas with us. Fortunately they got on a truck that was coming and papa met them at the crossroads. A heavy rain came so they had to sleep in the car that night. I was quite troubled when they did not come that evening. So I was happy when they came along at 9 o'clock in the morning. It was great to be together for Christmas again, since it was four years since the last time we could do so.

December 31. We were all set to go to Lebanon. We decided we would start out before breakfast so we could reach the highway by sun up, because we get the sun right smack in our eyes. The morning was cool and beautiful as we started out. We had twelve nice big chickens on top of the roof. We planned on having some chicken dinners together on Lebanon. After we had gone fifteen kilometers Papa remembered he had forgotten his hearing aid. How sad we were, but there was nothing to do but to turn back. So Carl and I stayed to make sandwiches for breakfast while papa and Folkvard returned to get the hearing aid. But they did not come back as expected. We waited and waited, but no car in sight. After a couple of hours we saw a white speck way off in the horizon. It was a person with a white cloth dangling in the wind. As he came nearer we saw he had white legs and then we knew something was up. They had a breakdown so Folkvard came back to tell us what happened. So papa walked to Bekily to get a truck. We all had to return to Bekily and start all over again.

January 8, 1946. A week later we started out again and arrived in Fort Dauphin about 3pm. We are beginning to think about sending Folkvard and Carl on the American boat which is to arrive in Tamatave about the first of February. Norlies and Rossings are there already waiting for the boat and it would mean a lot for us if our boys could travel with them. On January 15 Miss Bertha Rorstad, the boys' teacher for many years, gave a lovely graduation dinner, like a banquet.

January 16. A telegram came telling us that the boat is expected in Tamatave the 24th of January and is to depart the first of February. We hurried and packed food and clothing and went to town to make arrangements for the boys to leave. Gilbert Cabiro, nicknamed Cubby, is going to take our car and drive them to Betroka to catch the Trans-Sud which had already left Fort Dauphin earlier in the day. So now we have said goodbye to Folkvard and Carl. It all happened so fast. I had hoped to give a farewell dinner for them, but now we will have to eat all the chickens ourselves.

January 27. The Mission Conference opened this morning with twenty one men and women present. There was reading of reports all day; I got so tired of listening to them. One report is very much like the others. The crying need in all of them is a lack of workers, both missionaries and natives, and dilapidated buildings. But on the other hand, there is an increase in self-support and self-government, both good. We were given Beloha too, besides Bekily and Tsivory, to tend to. It will be a busy year for us.

February 10. The boys left Tamatave. By February 28 we had not heard any word from them.

March 23. We returned to Bekily after a fairly good vacation. We just received a letter from Arlene stating that she is engaged. The boys arrived in Minneapolis on March 14. Papa and I left for a long tour to Bekitro, Tranoroa, Beloha, and Belindo. We were gone nine days. It felt good to get home again, get a bath and sleep in a bed, after roughing it. We had to sleep on the floor and I can't say it was comfortable. We received more than enough milk, eggs and chickens, so we did not suffer from any lack of food.

On June 3 Arlene was married. We received a letter from Carl but have not heard from Folkvard for some time. Folkvard joined the army and Carl writes that Folkvard is learning demolition and how to use different kinds of explosives. It sounds dangerous to me. There are many who will have to sacrifice their lives on account of the war. Conditions in Europe and elsewhere are very serious. One might say the world is going on the rocks.

September 26. Papa was on his way to Fort Dauphin. After getting on the highway about 30 kilometers towards Antanimora, two tires blew out at the same time, the front one on the right side and the back one on the left side. The car swerved to one side into the ditch and tipped over with the wheels in the air. The front right fender and headlight, windshield, and the top of the car were crushed. After some time a truck came along and went on to Antanimora to get some tires for the car, so papa was able to get the car to Antanimora. After getting the car in shape good enough to run, he decided to return to Bekily. After going ten kilometers another tire blew out. He changed the tire and started off again, but after going a short distance, another blow out. Now he had no more tires to replace, so he continued to drive on the rim until he got within five kilometers from Beklily, when the rim was all gone. From there he drove on the hub, making that the hardest trip he ever had to make. That he was not hurt or killed was a miracle; we have much to be thankful for. Papa had to work a long time on the car with inadequate tools and spare parts.

We have been here seven years now and our thoughts are beginning to wander homeward.

March 10, 1947. It has been a long time since I wrote in my diary. We bade Bekily farewell the 8th of January and on the 9th we started out for Fort Dauphin. It felt kind of strange to leave Bekily for the third time. We feel as if we know every rock. Many of the workers expressed their sorrow over our leaving. The congregation came to bid us farewell and presented us with a gift of 710 francs, equal to about ten dollars. We will buy something as a remembrance of their thoughtfulness. We got our packing done nicely, but to find a truck to haul everything is a bigger problem. After waiting two whole months, a truck finally got scheduled.

At the Mission Conference a lot of attention was given to organizing the Malagasy Lutheran Church. The time has certainly come when the Malagasy Christians must take more responsibility in running the affairs of their church. They have reached the adult stage when they want to do things their way. The placing of missionaries was a problem, so few workers for so many demands. For that reason we were given a job as matron of the M. C. Home until Miss Nybroten returns from furlough. We hope to leave in May or June. So here we are settled in the matron's room, the room that Miss Celia Thompson occupied for so many years. I feel this is quite a big responsibility at this time, because we are both fatigued. We have been here one week and have tried to get well trained for the task before Miss Olson leaves.

June 2 is our 25th wedding anniversary. We have done nothing to celebrate. We hope we can have a memorial day with our dear ones at home this time of the year. We are still at the M. C. Home preparing for our departure for America. We had our big sale a week ago. Practically everything went over the top, as the saying goes. I gave up my job as matron to Evelyn a week ago. It was a good experience for me. I can appreciate so much more now what Miss Thompson did during the many years she was in charge here. Kittel and Anna and Alice arrived from America two weeks ago, so we have had some interesting visits with them. Papa plans to go to Tananarive on the Trans-Sud this week, but the bus has not come yet.

I have not written about the uprising here on the island. A political party was organized some time ago working for independence for Madagascar. Last year the French agreed to let the natives choose their own delegates to go to Tananarive and also to Paris. These delegates traveled by plane and each time that one came to visit, they were royally received by the natives. Everybody went out to greet them. Well, things seemed to be going along fine. The natives were given more rights and responsibilities. At the beginning of this year we heard rumors that there were other plans underneath. This party had made plans to overthrow the French government, kill all the white people and take over. It is hard to imagine or believe that the natives here would do such a thing. It was reported that cases of documents were found and telegrams were intercepted that indicated that these were not only rumors but really true. A certain night was set for the attack throughout the island. The French in Fort Dauphin were all inside the Fort for several nights. Fortunately the government here got hold of the plans, so they placed guards at strategic places. A search was made and all who had been active were put in prison. Pastor Gilbert and Jonarivelo from our church were delegates and resigned from the mission work. So they were among those taken to prison. They say that Rateaver had also been involved. In many places the attacks were successful and many people, both French and Malagasy, were killed. Towns have been razed to the ground. Many cruel killings have been reported and the war is going on up north along the coast. A number of soldiers, both French and Sinegalese, have arrived to clean up the infected districts. We have much to be thankful for that people here have been spared a massacre.

June 11. Papa left for Tananarive today. We have not heard from him yet. Over a week after he left, I received a telegram that he arrived safely. Here are a few headlines about the rebellion. The first visible attack was on the 10th of May, 1946, in Tananarive when rocks began to fly in the streets. The rebels had a plot to overthrow the government and kill all the French on the night of March 29, 1947. This was reported in the newspaper, *La Lumière*. They stated that all whites were to be killed. Raseta is the number one leader; Rabemananjara number two; and Ravoahangy number three. Raseta was to be the delegate to France and the other two the highest authorities in Tananarive. Two thousand arrests were made. Thousands of natives have been killed, and at least 180 French. The big plantation owners have lost everything and some of them killed. Some of the women and children have not been found yet. The government is getting reinforcements and the doctor here volunteered his services with the paratroopers. The French really have a job on their hands and have no reason to be optimistic about the situation.

July 26. After saying goodbye to our friends in Fort Dauphin, we took the plane for Tamatave. The vibration and swaying made me sick, so I did not enjoy the plane ride. When we arrived we found that every hotel in town was filled. A ship had just arrived with 3000 soldiers to fight the rebels here. And hundreds of French women and children came here to board the ships leaving for France. Ducommen was kind enough to send us to the French Mission, so here we are with Miss Benoit, the teacher at the school. There is no hope for passage now, but we can get our baggage on the John P. Mitchel steamship direct for New York. Tamatave is a much bigger city than I imagined it to be. There are many beautiful homes and large yards with luxurious flower gardens. On Sunday we attended both French and Malagasy church services. The church is large and so is the attendance, 400 communicant members.

August 2. We took a plane to Tananarive. Rev. Buchsenschutz met us and took us to his home. We hope we can take a plane to Paris next Sunday, but we are waiting word from Paris about possible connections to New York.

August 10. We went to church this morning. Well, here we will be for some days. No passage on the plane from Paris to New York can be had before October. We were very disappointed. We asked the American Consul to telegraph Cairo for possible passage. We hope and pray for a favorable answer. The past week has been very interesting. The market place has so many things to buy; our pocket book is getting thin. The wood carvings and paintings have been most attractive. We have bought eleven paintings (150 francs each) and a pair of book ends (300 francs).

August 11. A telegram came saying we have plane passage for August 28. Good news! We leave here one week from tomorrow. We left Tananarive on August 24 at 5:30am by plane and got to French Africa for lunch. Flying is a wonderful experience. The roar of the engine is terrific and it is quite impossible to sleep. When we got above the clouds, it seemed like we were in another world. When we arrived in Khartoum, we were whizzed away to a hotel. It is hot in Africa now but comfortable in the hotel. The supper and breakfast were fine. The African servants were very quick and able. The next morning they brought us tea and then we were off to the airport again. There was no stop until we got to Cairo. We followed the Nile River for many miles. We saw the pyramids and big sand dunes. What a desert! We did not fly high as there were no clouds. After landing in Cairo, we felt like lost birds as Air France did not take care of us anymore. Fortunately, the agent for the Jollie Company met us and took us to a hotel. He helped us in every way and the next day he went with papa to see about further passage and to get money. On account of his efficient help we got passage to leave the 27th at noon. Hence, we were in Cairo for only a day and a half.

August 27. We left by plane at noon and arrived in Athens, Greece, at 5:45pm. Here we had supper and found the Greek cooking very good. This being an American plane, we noticed a different kind of service. Gum, cakes and orangeade, books, writing paper, and cold water were passed around. Everything to make the passengers comfortable was offered. At 11pm we arrived in Rome and left at midnight. At 4 o'clock we arrived in Gevena. Here we had lunch. At each stop we were allowed to step off for an airing. About 7am we arrived in Paris but we did not see much of it, not enough to make us feel that we were in the big city.

They herded us into a crowded lunch room and locked us in. Some of the passengers got sore. We were in there for an hour or more.

August 28 we arrived in Shannon, Ireland, at 10am. Here we had a good dinner. We left at 11 o'clock. The air here is very fresh and the country side is beautiful. Because of bad weather we have to go south to the Azores. We landed there at 6pm. We landed in Newfoundland at midnight. Here we had breakfast — Shredded Wheat, stewed prunes, bacon and eggs and real coffee. August 29 we landed in Boston because of the fog and rain in New York. It certainly feels good to get our feet on the soil of U.S.A. We arrived in New York at 9am and had no trouble with papa's visa or baggage. We even got a check cashed so we had money for a taxi. We got in touch with the Deaconess Home and were happy when we were able to get a clean room there with bath and comfortable beds. We enjoyed the security of being in a Christian home and felt very fortunate.

August 30. This morning papa and I started out on the subway to find the office where we could buy our tickets. By early afternoon we were on the train to Chicago. How fine the coaches are. We decided not to reserve a berth this time, but to sleep in the seat with a pillow. The next morning we arrived in Chicago at 9am and hurried to get tickets for Minneapolis. We checked our baggage and barely got to the train on time. We enjoyed the train ride. The farms and villages looked prosperous. We sent a telegram from Chicago so that Glen and Augusta Norton would meet us. How good it was to see them. Our long journey was finally at an end. It really was a wonderful journey and we are thankful to God for His wonderful protection.

We went to the Nortons for the night. Augusta had a good dinner waiting for us. What a treat to get a home cooked meal again. Rybergs were at their cottage in Lake Koronis, but came along the following day. The same evening Arlene called from Kansas City. And the next morning Carl called Augusta to ask if there was any news from us. How happy he was when I came to the phone. A couple of days later Agnes and Folkvard also called. It was thrilling to hear our dear ones again. The first thing we did was to get some clothes and go to the Mission office to learn where we might live on furlough. We were so happy to learn that we could live in the Mission Cottage in Northfield where the boys will be going to St. Olaf College.

On October 20 Agnes came with Gloria to visit. How grand it is to meet again after seven and a half years of separation. On Christmas Eve Arlene and Jim arrived at 6:30am. How wonderful to have them with us for Christmas. We have it nice and comfortable here in Northfield and we like it very much. We would like to settle down here for good. We had our Christmas party with Glen and Augusta Norton and with Clarence and Olga Ryberg and Kenneth's family.

1948. Papa had an operation at the Mayo Clinic in April so he was at the hospital during Holy Week and Easter. Agnes, Gloria, Arlene and Jim arrived here after Easter. Agnes spent one month and Arlene two months with us. Papa and I spent six days with Clarence and Olga Ryberg at their cottage in Lake Koronis. It was a wonderful week, so restful and peaceful. Olga and I had some nice walks along the roadside. We enjoyed the boat rides on the lake.

In September we made a trip to Texas to visit Agnes, over 1000 miles. We enjoyed so much meeting Bill, Agnes' husband, whom we had not met. I made a trip to Inwood, Iowa, to visit the Moens, Arlene's in-laws. I also visited Sioux Falls, Canton, and Minneapolis. I also made a trip to St. Cloud to visit my friends Stella and Ole. I also visited my old friend, Minnie Snesrud, in Webster one weekend. Papa made a two-week tour to Denver. Arlene also spent one week with us in September at the time of my birthday, 54 years old I am. My family gave me twelve trays, something I have really wished for.

June 2. Jim and Arlene were here for our wedding anniversary, 27 years. They gave us a pressure cooker which is a real addition to my cooking utensils. The boys have done well in their freshman year of college and are both on the honor roll. Valborg graduated from college so we had quite a reunion at our house. We have enjoyed the many concerts at St. Olaf College and most of all living here in Northfield to have the boys living with us. I have also enjoyed meeting so many fine people here. Mission Retreat was held at St. Olaf. The weather was ideal and the program was well carried out. It was interesting to meet so many missionaries from the various fields. I entertained the Mission Society. It was fun to prepare for Christmas, to go shopping, wrapping gifts, and do the baking for it. We had a fine Christmas party at the Rybergs. Glennora and family, the Nortons and we were there. Then we had a party with Hazel, Arndt, and Valborg, and lastly on Christmas Eve for ourselves. Valborg spent her whole vacation with us.

January 16, 1949. Randall James, Arlene's son, was born at 4pm in Aberdeen, South Dakota. Everything went fine and we are happy for that. I went up there the next Sunday. Arlene got home at 2pm and I arrived at 4pm. It was a new experience for me to play the part of grandma in the care of a new born baby. Papa and I both had thorough physical exams. If there was any ailment, they sure should be able to find it. We are to go back to Dr. Ylvisaker in a few weeks to get the results. So whether we pass or not will decide our future.

April 17. Easter Sunday. We have had a quiet day. Little did we know what would happen in our family before the day was past. At 10pm we got a telephone call from Agnes in Texas that Bill had been in a car accident and was in critical condition. At once we made plans that I should go to Texas to be with them, but we hoped that we would get better news. The next morning Agnes called and said that Bill had passed away. Poor Agnes! How our hearts ached for her. And what can we do to help? Agnes would be alone with a small child to support. The Mahoneys took care of all the expenses for the funeral. I went to be with Agnes and took charge of the kitchen and did all the packing to get Agnes ready to leave Texas. Bill's funeral was beautiful and he was given a nice place in Austin Memorial Cemetery. The pastor was very helpful and so were his many friends, especially the Highway Department for which Bill had worked. Agnes and Bill had just had their church membership transferred the Sunday before and on Easter Sunday they both had received Holy Communion. Several of Bill's relatives had spent the afternoon with them and Bill had seemed unusually happy. Only a couple of hours later the accident happened. Bill had many friends and they all spoke very highly of him. God bless his memory and help Agnes and Gloria in their struggle.

June 13. We moved into our own house on Orchard Street. We paid $9000 for it plus $500 for new plumbing. Papa painted the house and garage. We like this place and find it homelike.

September 1. August has been a busy month as we have been preparing to return to Madagascar. The summer passed by so quickly. Agnes, Gloria and I spent a few days with Olga at Lake Koronis. We had a reunion at Glenora's house on Sunday. The Mission Society gave us a nice send off by having Open House at our house. They presented us with a purse of $35.50. On this day papa and Folkvard arrived in New York with the car. They had a good trip with no mishap. I went by train and had a nice visit with Sister Anna and Sister Mette. We are staying at Prince George Hotel in NewYork. I arrived here on Fokvard's birthday, September 5. He stayed with Papa until I arrived. After dinner he and I took a long bus ride up 5th Avenue and along the River Boulevard. When we returned it was time for him to leave. He took the Trail Blazer. This morning papa and I went to the docks and in the afternoon we went to Montgomery Ward by metro. We bought a bed with spring and mattress, $44.66.

On September 13 we got on the Robin Kirk with all our bags and baggage and departed at 1:20pm. As we left we could see the Statue of Liberty which is always a welcome sight. The food on the boat is good and we eat more than we should. In a week we will be in Capetown. We are enjoying this trip, the weather is good and I am reading some good books.

September 29. Happy birthday to me! We hope to have an interesting visit in Capetown. Two passengers will leave us here. We will be only eight of us left. We arrived in Capetown October 3. This is a very beautiful harbor. The Table Mountain is in the background and the city lies beneath it. At night it looks like an amphitheater with its lights sloping up the mountainside. Yesterday we took the bus to Park Kransbrosch. It's the most beautiful park we have ever seen. It is springtime here and the flowers are in their most beautiful stage of bloom. We had coffee and scones in the Tea House in the sun. I never thought the air could be so cool in Africa. They have the most beautiful homes and gardens.

We left Capetown yesterday at 10am and arrived at Port Elizabeth at 2pm today. This city is built on solid rocky cliffs, so there is not much vegetation. Snake Park and museum are here where the serum for snake bites is made. We visited the museum and found it very interesting. We took the bus to one end of town where the beach and hotels are. Since this is Sunday we went to a Presbyterian Church. They had a service in honor of the Mayor. The judge was there with his curly wig and the mayor in his bright red robe. We were too late for dinner, so we browsed around in the cupboard and found something to eat — a whole delicious coconut pie.

Just finished reading the Five Books of Moses. The ship has been unloading cars and spare parts. Now they are loading cars for Durban. On October 13 we arrived in East London, a beautiful city. The streets are wide and clean. It lies very high above the pier. We only took a walk through the town. We arrived in Durban the next day at 10am. We got off shore and went to the Swedish Mission Home. We visited some of the Lutheran missionaries here in South Africa. We saw the first mission station started by Bishop Schröder eighty years ago. The house and church were built by him. Elephants and other wild animals used to prowl around the grounds. We will never forget the hairpin bends on the road and the speed which seemed too scary for us.

October 30. We are leaving Durban at 5pm today. We have enjoyed our stay in Durban very much. The hospitality at Svenskbo made us feel at home. Durban is a beautiful city and the stores are full of goods like any city in the USA. We arrived in Lorenzo Marques on November 1. We went down town this morning and bought a helmet for papa. From here we are heading directly for Fort Dauphin. That is what we had hoped for; now it seems almost too good to be true.

On November 5 we anchored just outside of Fort Dauphin because the sea was rough. The captain did not want to spend any time in Fort Dauphin. We managed to get our baggage off but we could not get on land, so we had to go along to Tamatave. In Tamatave we stayed with a

French missionary for fourteen days. We finally got the import license for the car which we had brought along from the States. We got our car off the boat and then drove to Tananarive. We had been warned that the roads were bad; it turned out they were worse than we expected. We stayed in Tananarive for a day and a half to get gas, money, and rest up.

We left for Antsirabe at 7pm and arrived at Hotel Commerce at 11:30pm. We visited the Norwegian Mission and enjoyed our half day here. Next day we left for Fianarantsoa and arrived at 2pm.

On November 30 we arrived in Fort Dauphin. We realize and acknowledge how wonderful the Lord has kept us well all the way. We hope and pray that we might be of service in the Lord's kingdom again this term. We are now with Kittel and Anna for a couple of days. On December we got our baggage through customs and all the red tape. Yesterday we had turkey dinner with the Munsons. Tomorrow we go to Lebanon to unpack. Fever has started again to pester me, so I had to start taking the cure again. We went to Kittel and Anna for Christmas. They had a nice tree and we had a good supper with them. I was sick in bed all Christmas Day. After that I started getting better day by day.

A year ago it seemed strange to think about 1950. Now it is a reality. How much has happened the past year. What this coming year has in store for us we do not know, but we always look forward to the new year with high hopes and resolutions. May our fourth term be a fruitful one for the Lord's work. All the missionaries are here now for the Annual Conference. We had three and a half weeks of conference. In March we leave for Tsihombe where we have been placed for this term. Our children at home are all well, happy, and busy. We are happy for that. We found the house in Tsihombe very dusty. This is a good house, the latest model out here. Petera who was born and raised here is my cook and his 15 year old daughter my house girl. We like it here. It really is a nicer location than Behara or Bekily where we have been before. The air is better too, since we are only thirty kilometers from the ocean.

May 1, 1950. By this time we are as settled as ever we will be. We had the cistern scrubbed today. We just made a tour to Beloha for three days.

Papa went to Ampotaka also, in all 129 miles of driving. We enjoyed our visits except for the bats. Their stink can turn anyone's stomach.

May 25. We just had visitors, Sister Laura, Lyla Sivesind, and the American Consul. During vacation Kittel and Anna visited us for a week. We went to Behara for the Annual District Conference and had a good meeting, with cordial hospitality. The Ruuds, Sister Laura, and Bertha Rorstad were also there. After Sunday we drove to Fort Dauphin and Anna filled my tooth. Four weeks ago a thief broke into our house while we were in church and stole 7,500 francs. The first night after we left for Behara, the same one broke in again and brought back the car keys which had been stolen three weeks before during noon hour. The cook is the guilty party, if not he, then his son. There are so many evidences to that effect that there can be no doubt. We have talked to him twice but he refuses to admit his guilt. Now the government is working on it. We had to fire the cook, Petera, a week ago because we are convinced he is the thief. Since having no cook now, it has been a tough week. I got a bad attack of stomach trouble that left me so weak.

December 22. The time is already approaching Christmas. I have made candy for all the sub-stations and for here in town too, three big wash dishes full. The cook, the suspected thief, was called to Ambovombe for the second time to answer questions. Will he be found guilty or not?

Our children are fine. Agnes, Folkie, and Carl have only one semester left at St. Olaf College before graduation. In her last letter Agnes announced her engagement to Leonard Akland. Our very best wishes go with them. Agnes is in the St. Olaf Choir this year. She was also among the few chosen to be on the Senior Musical Recital. Good for her! We are happy too that Folkvard and Carl are doing so well. They have been on the Honor Roll every year.

We have had a quiet Christmas with only the regular routine work. On January 3, 1951 we arrived in Fort Dauphin and Lebanon. The truck that is bringing our baggage got stalled because of the flood and did not arrive until four days later. I have no cook but I have Vao who is better than any boy. Every house on Lebanon is filled now with the arrival of new missionaries. In 1946 there was not a single child on Lebanon and now there are thirty.

A storm began on the 29th of January and continued raining for four days. Anyone who lived through that will never forget it. The government sent out a word of warning that a cyclone was coming and everyone should prepare for it. The Missionary Conference was at the M. C. Home and they were warned too. Papa decided not to take his car to the Conference in Fort Dauphin and got a ride with someone else. As soon as the warning came, the Conference was dismissed and everyone hurried home. But before we could get to Lebanon, the storm was already hitting us. The rain came in torrents and the wind in gusts so strong that we were afraid to leave our house. In the afternoon I looked out toward the garage and saw the garage door swinging back and forth. So I called papa to go out and see. It was not the garage door at all but the whole front wall. But before he got there the corner post of the garage where our car stood had broken and the heavy slate roof was resting on top of the car. A big dent was made on top of the roof and both front wind shields were smashed into thousands of pieces. The neighbors helped to raise the roof and got the car out. The next morning the garage was flat on the ground. The first night our house was wet too except where we had our beds. The wind was so strong it tore away every branch of the trees around us. We were afraid some of the big trees would come smashing down on our house. The ocean was terrifying and we were filled with anxiety. Practically every roof of the French homes and of the new hospital was stripped away and lay open to the rains for four days. All the trees on Lebanon were made bare of their leaves. A lot of the native huts fell flat to the ground. In Androy there were big lakes where one never saw water otherwise. One of our sub-stations, Imonga, was many feet under water and the people had to flee to higher ground in the middle of the night. Every living thing was drowned.

March 17. Our vacation ended and we arrived in Tsihombe at noon. With our broken windshields it was difficult for papa to see the road. March 23 is Good Friday, a week since we arrived. Our house got wet because of the storm and the walls and furniture are covered with mold.

The floors are swollen from the water. Minor damages have been done to the houses here so there will be a lot of work for the carpenters. But good workers are scarce around here.

September 2. Last week we attended the Annual Conference in Ambovombe. We had ideal weather; the attendance was good and the programs were carried out very well. We stayed with the Ruuds. After the meetings were over, we drove on to Fort Dauphin. I had several teeth filled by Anna and spent a lot of money as we usually do when we go to town. At any rate I got the fridge full of vegetables. It feels good to have something in the cupboard.

On September 15 we had visitation at all our substations led by Rev. Munson. I went along to Beloha and stayed over night. Today I feel like yelling a loud "Hurrah!" We finished a big job in the house which makes the rooms look like a palace compared to what they were before. Papa was able to mix the paint with various shades that are soft and pleasing to look at. We still have the office left and the upstairs to do. This week we have our Six Months Meeting so we will not get anything done for now.

December 30. We have had an unusual hot December without rain. Never have we felt the heat so intense as this year. For that reason we left Tsihombe December 27 for Lebanon. The heavy rains might begin any day and we hate to get caught in rain and mud. We have no glass in the side front door and our brakes are dead. We arrived in Fort Dauphin in the morning and had dinner with Kittel and Anna.

New Year's Eve we were with Alton Halvorsens and Tosos at Laurel Johnsons for a little while and had watermelon, saw some moving pictures and had devotions together. At the Mission Conference in January we were given Antanimora to take care of, so now we have three stations. Papa had a big job done on the car to fix the brakes and windshields. We arrived safe and sound at Tsihombe and it feels good to be back. I am always nervous when we go over the mountain of Mahatsentsona and so relieved when we get across it. The turns are so sharp and the embankments so steep that they scare me. We look forward to a successful year of work. We are both in good health. We have three new catechists to join our staff. With both Beloha and Antanimora we will be busy. There has been a heavy rain up north which is keeping the river filled up so we have not been able to get across to Beloha. We finally made our visit to Beloha for three days and Antanimora for two days this month.

September 4. We drove to Tsivory to attend the 50th anniversary of the mission work there. The fine weather made our visit pleasant. The programs and attendance were good. Laurel Johnson is stationed there. Alton Halvorson, Anna Braaten, Eleonor Johnson and Judith Knutson came out to help on the programs.

December 25. Christmas Day. We are having a happy season. Wilfred, the pastor, preached a good sermon, "Jesus, the Gift." We also attended the children's program as usual. The kids have been working so hard the last month and each one had so many parts. I don't see how the little ones can remember all they do. I gave a party for the catechists. I had the tree up and trimmed. I served cool aid, cake and candies. Then I gave a party for the Preparatory School pupils in their classroom. I showed flannel graph of the Christmas story. I did the same for Gilbert's class. About sixty attended. The next thing on our program is to get ready to go to Lebanon.

Kittel and Anna left by plane for America January 9, 1953. Another of the missionary old-timers gone. It seems sad to see them leave the work which has been so much a part of them, but such is life. So we pass the oars to the younger ones who are coming to take our places. We are all ready to go out to our stations. We have finished packing, the truck comes tomorrow and we hope to leave on Tuesday. We have had a good vacation and a good conference, lasting only eight days. The Bible Study was led by Leo Lellelid and was very good.

March 3. We were hoping to return to Tsihombe, but we got word that the ferry at Amboasary with two cars on it was carried down the river in a torrent of water coming like a wall. One was Bougroff's new car. How relieved we are that we did not go. So here we are staying put for a while.

On March 13 we finally got a truck to take our baggage, so we started out this morning in pouring rain. It continued to rain all the way and the roads were bad. We finally made it home safely, so thankful.

May 10. We were invited to Tranoroa so papa could help Vern Toso decide what to do about the church as it needs a major repair job. Papa preached the sermon even though he felt sick. The people in Tranoroa were happy to see us again, but there were so few left of the old timers.

June 2. This is our 31st wedding anniversary. We had a quiet day; all the workers were off because of a funeral. Our special treat today was ice cream, which we never had in our former days in Madagascar. Something new has happened. Fort Dauphin now has electric lights around town and on the streets, a good sign of progress. New buildings are also being erected.

February 21, 1954. We had ten sessions of Conference but no Synod Regional (the Malagasy responsibility for their church) due to failures of most stations to meet their self-support. However, Tsihombe, Beloha, and Antanimora met theirs as well as Manafiafy. Gunda Hennum was moved to Tsihombe, so now our Primary School will be able to open again after being closed for five years due to lack of teachers. We are also getting a pastor for the district of Faux Cap. Our annual welcome and farewell party among our missionaries was unusually good. A clever play by the Old Maids Club was given by those going home and recently arrived. Now we are getting ready to return to the station but papa has a sore foot, so swollen he cannot get his shoe on. The swelling does not seem to go down. This is the third day. There are no mangos to purchase at the market but loads of pineapples. Meat is scarce, but plenty of chickens. I have two hens laying eggs. One egg costs 10 francs.

March 6. There has been a lot of rain up north and all the rivers are very high. Rossings have been sitting in Bekily a week without being able to get across the river. We also have been waiting, but it is a blessing in disguise for us because papa's foot is still very sore. But the truck came this morning and we had a merry chase to get all our baggage on it.

May 5. Our Primary School is in full swing now after having been closed for five years. It is a big satisfaction to see so many children attending. This school continues to be our bright spot here in Tsihombe. Papa was in Antanimora alone last week. On his way home he got stuck in a ravine, a detour as they were putting in a new bridge. The government workers had filled this with sand and had let it stay that way. This was Saturday, so they had gone home for the week end. Papa dug in the sand for more than an hour. Finally a truck came along and pulled him out.

July 13. This is a busy year. We are in Antanimora one week and the next in Tsihombe. The masonry of the new church is coming up slowly. One side is up over the arches, but now we have only two masons. Workers come and go. When they make enough money for taxes, they don't care to work any more. Why work if you are not in a pinch? We are going to Fort Dauphin tomorrow. Papa has to buy building materials. When we arrived in Fort Dauphin, we were invited to stay with the Hofstads, even though we had planned on camping in Lebanon. We got our shopping done in several days so we left for Ambovombe, stayed over night with the Stolees, went to church, had dinner with them and left for home (Tsihombe) at 3pm.

September 4. Arndt and Hazel and children came from Tananarive. They have just signed on to be missionaries here. Arndt grew up here as a boy and is now returning as a missionary. It was so much fun to see them. Mehls and Olsons also came as new missionaries, quite a reinforcement.

September 11. It is papa's 66th birthday. We had our circuit meeting in Ambovombe with an immense crowd. On Saturday evening there was no meeting, so all the missionaries, Laura Olson, Sister Alene, Stolees, Torviks and we, were invited to Sister Laura's and Laila Anderson's house for supper. Mrs. Stolee made the birthday cake and served with ice cream. They all sang "Happy Birthday" for Dad. He did not seem to know it was his birthday, so he was taken by surprise when we sang his name.

October 8. Papa has been up on the roof of the church and out in the sun all day long, so he is sun burnt and feels uncomfortable. This forenoon he used the torch and bent the iron bars which hold the rafters on to the wall. No strong wind will now be able to tear them off. The mason is working on the front gable and tomorrow papa hopes to raise the cross on it. The carpenters are finishing the joists. Papa is pushing the masons and carpenters all he can to finish the job. The carpenters are now putting on the iron roofing. But papa had a great disappointment this morning, when they were to put toll on the second side. They had not put the joists the same distance apart as on the first side, so the toll did not reach. Francois, the one who is supposed to be the head carpenter, is so dense, he can never follow measurements.

Today the roof was finished, after a week of disappointments. When we returned on Tuesday, we learned that Francois had skipped town after he received his pay on Friday evening. He stole a bicycle and went to Isonala to sell it. He left with debts around town with eighteen people amounting to 11,500 francs. We have known that he is dishonest, but we never dreamed he was such a big thief. He has stolen boards here, made small tables and sold them. Papa ran short of tolls for the iron roofing, so he telegraphed Fort Dauphin to send out 50 tolls at two and a half meters. When they arrived, they were only two meters. So he telegraphed to Tsihombe and asked for 50 tolls from the Mission supply as soon as possible. The third day they arrived. It was blazing hot so dad got sun burnt again and his legs are bruised. He is awfully hard on himself. But if he had not pitched in the way he did, the work on the building would not have progressed so far. What a relief when the roof was finished without any mishap. Dad has been climbing up on those rafters like a monkey. Too much for a man of his age.

December 25. Christmas Day! First we had a Christmas party for the Preparatory School students. I presented the Christmas story with the flannel board, gave out candy and peanuts, and marched around the Christmas tree. Then Thursday evening we had our own little celebration. This same evening there was the most beautiful rainbow we have ever seen. It was so bright and evenly colored from one horizon to the other. Mail is stalled somewhere it seems, because we have not received a Christmas greeting from any of our children.

We are planning our trip to Lebanon for vacation. The truck left on Monday and we left on Wednesday and arrived in Fort Dauphin at 10:30am. We had dinner with Hazel, supper with Stolees, and dinner the next day with Hofstads. In the afternoon all the missionaries were invited for a birthday party for Rev. Hofstad. By New Year's Eve we are all settled in. We got our curtains hung today and washed all the floors and windows. We finally got Christmas greetings from Agnes and Carl. Agnes and Leonard have settled in Canton, South Dakota, where he will work as a doctor in a medical clinic. Agnes is happy about it. They had quite a job to find housing, but they are making the best of what they can find. Both Tack and Carl are planning to visit Agnes during the Christmas season. Agnes wrote, "If Arlene could come too, it would be perfect."

This New Year's Eve we look back on the past year as a very busy and strenuous one. We acknowledge that our Lord has been merciful and good to us. And we thank Him for all His guidance. We will continue to pray for His care also this coming year and for blessing the work we plan to do.

February 21. Well, here it is time to pack up and return to the station. We had one week of Regional Synod meeting, two weeks of the Missionary Conference, women's Bible study, farewell and welcome party, one outing with Hallangers and Arndts to Loftsinanana, all of which kept us busy. We have also had several picnic suppers with Arndt and Hazel. Once we drove out to Manantantely, Nampoana, and three times to the sea in different places. We are expecting a new pastor in Tsihombe. The truck came this evening to get our baggage. I have four fillings to put into my teeth. I cannot wear my partial plate anymore.

February 25. We returned to Tsihombe and are glad to be back and get ready for the work ahead of us. This will be our last full year, as we will be here for only five months the following year. Our baggage finally came yesterday so we are all settled in this evening. Both of us are tired with all this moving around and getting settled.

May 14. I am beginning to plan for the Annual District Meeting. If all come we will be 13 adults and 5 children — John Mehls, Laura Olson, Alene Smith, Laura Pederson, Laila Anderson, Stolees, and Ruuds. We have killed three turkeys, made a double batch of donuts, honey cookies, fruit cake, sponge cake, etc. I am feeling fine so I expect I will be able to manage all the hosting. Everyone we expected came except Sister Laura and Laila Anderson because they had bad colds. Dr. and

Mrs. Bolstad brought five visitors, native evangelists from the inland, who stayed here over night until the following day for dinner. We were then eighteen people.

The program for the meetings was rich in content and most of the speakers were excellent. Mr. Jonarivelo, the Synod President, was also with us and he gave a couple of good messages. I attended only four sessions because I did not want to overload myself. Both Ruuds and Stolees brought their cooks and that was a big help. With my boy, Calvin, we got along wonderfully. Gunda Hennum was in charge of the tables and that was a big relief. Dad has been Circuit President for five years and this will be his last here in Madagascar. Pastor Johnson gave a nice talk of appreciation for what we have done. He mentioned the many stations where we have worked. He asked the audience to sing, "Oh, happy day when we shall stand." It was very impressive to me. Dad gave a few words in response to the farewell talk and thanked them so much for their kind thoughts.

September 15. We have spent two weeks away from home, eleven days in Manambaro and three days in Manantantely with Arndt and Hazel. Dad had an inflammation in his right thigh called thrombosis phlebitis, that is, an inflammation of the vein. It is hard like a pencil. He stayed in bed for a whole week to let the vein heal. The work in Antanimora was too hard on him. He tends to overwork when he is at it.

Oliver Carlson grew up as a boy in Madagascar. Now he is returning to be a missionary like his father who died out here. On September 24 we were greatly surprised when our American visitors came here just as we had finished dinner. They were Dr. Syrdal, the executive secretary of the Mission Board, Rev. Friske, Rev. Hofstad, Tosos and Connie Lovaas. We expected them on Saturday but here they came on Friday. Fortunately I had fish on ice so we fried that, and together with rice, peas, and carrots we had plenty to serve them. And we had preserved peaches for dessert.

On September 25 we dedicated the new church in Amboasary. Dad has been working hard to get the new windshields into the car, but they turned out to be too large. In the effort to force them in, they cracked. How disgusting! Big expense for nothing!

December 8, 1955. This has been a very dry year. We had to buy two tons of rice and manioc to have available for the workers. There is no food except for what is shipped in. We have only two weeks before Christmas, so we have been writing cards and letters. We have had a good year in our work, with a big gain in statistics and we also met our goal for self-support. We had a fine Christmas season. The Sunday School children's program on Christmas Eve was very well prepared. On Christmas Day Pastor Elon Renaka and family and Emile Rakotosolo and Estera and six children visited. I served cocoa and *julekake*. Emile and Estera gave us a beautiful piece of embroidery. We had services this morning and in the afternoon we were busy packing to get our baggage ready to leave tomorrow.

New Years Day, 1956. We arrived in Lebanon for this year's vacation in time for lunch. For supper we were invited to Dr. Borges and the next day for dinner with the Hofstads. Dad has worked many days on door locks and windows in the apartment where we are living now on Lebanon. We have scrubbed and waxed the floors. We have begun to feel settled. Arndt and Hazel dropped in for coffee with us. We are both as well as can be and we are thankful for that.

January 22. The Conference began today. Duane Olson preached and Oliver Carlson conducted the liturgy. The missionary choir sang two songs. The theme was the grace of God in Christ. The first day of the Conference Hazel was to leave for Tananarive for her confinement. It was decided that Rev. Jacobson would take our place in Tsihombe, Norli goes to Beloha and Knutson to Manamabaro. So now we have three missionaries to replace us at the three stations for which we were responsible.

Arndt was in Tananarive when Hazel took sick, so we have Linda and Evangeline with us. Hazel was in Fort Dauphin a whole week and then they took her to Tananarive and operated the same day. They delivered her baby by Caesarian Section. We got a telegram saying everything is okay.

February 5. We just returned from the mission cemetery. We had not been there for several years. There are nineteen graves there. Sorry to see that it is not kept up. Weeds are five feet high. I am surprised to see what a simple stone we have to honor the memory of Miss Dahl. We are ready to have our sale, but we have to wait until the Conference is over. Arndt will return on Friday, so he can be present too. Dad has a bad cold. He preached in Fort Dauphin last Sunday and barely made it through. Linda and Evangeline are still in our care. Arndt has been placed in Manantantely. Dad had a spell of weakness and is getting hypos of vitamin B. We are all ready to leave but we are waiting for the truck, which is a good thing because Dad is not ready to travel. The truck came at 8am the next day for our baggage and four tons of rice. So we got busy to load our car, ate a little and were ready to leave Fort Dauphin at 11am. It got cloudy for our travel which was a great relief. Amboasary was difficult as usual. Two big trucks were stuck in the sand on the other side. When could we expect to get across the river? We finally got across easier than we expected. We were thankful for the clouds because most of the time the sun is so bright it blinds the driver. We found a dirty house here as we always do when we return from Lebanon. The next day we were both so exhausted, so we went to bed at 6:30 and did not get up unto 6:30 the next morning. When I got up, my girl Vao was on the veranda telling me her sister Hely, who served so faithfully for several years, had died during the night. She was unconscious when they first noticed that something was wrong and she never came to consciousness again. Poor girl. She had been to the hospital to have her baby and had been home only three days. Vao who works for me now has three children and a younger sister had a baby last fall.

March 17. We received a letter from Rugtveit telling us that Hans, dad's oldest brother, had died February 22, 1956. He had been very feeble for more than a year and had been at an Old People's Home for three years or more. Since Olav is 71 years old now, Hans must have been at least 73 years old. We also received a letter saying that cousin Emma Titrud passed away after having a stroke.

March 23. There is famine in south Madagascar. The crops have all dried up because of no rain. Hundreds of people have left for other parts of the island. Those who have money can buy food, but those who have no money eat cooked cactus leaves. A lot of young men have left their families to find work, hoping to send money back home.

We are ready to say farewell to Tsihombe and Antanimora. Another milestone past. Exactly one month from today we will be in Paris. June 2 is our 34th anniversary, and that is how long it has been since we left the USA for Madagascar. Tonight is our last night in Tsihombe. We can hardly realize that is true. Yesterday the congregation had a short farewell program. Filipo Rajoela recited a short poem; the pastor said a few words, several songs were sung, and after that the whole congregation came up to the station to say farewell. And they presented us with a lunch cloth and six napkins. Rajaona Marie represented the congregation with a brief talk of thanks and appreciation for our work. It was all nicely planned and we feel that they meant it. This evening Pastor Elon Renaka and family came to say goodbye. He read the 23rd Psalm. We appreciate their visit.

June 10. This is our last Sunday here in Madagascar. We had a wonderful church service in Fort Dauphin. Hofstad preached a sermon on the theme, "The True Church," which had also been the theme throughout the three days of meetings. The church was packed. To us it was an especially solemn service, knowing that it was to be our last time to worship with the natives and our co-workers. In the afternoon we had service with Communion, and Arndt preached the sermon, the first time we heard him preach. This service was also very impressive and beautiful. At the end of the afternoon service Pastor Johnson Ramiandrazo gave a short farewell talk of appreciation for the many years of service we have devoted to this work. Dad responded with a word of admonition and the hope of the living church. We appreciated the farewell they gave even though we have never served in Fort Dauphin. In the evening every one of the missionaries gathered at Carlson's home in Lebanon for a potluck supper and we were the honored guests.

June 11. I am spending this day at the home of Arndt and Hazel while dad and Arndt went to town to finish up some business affairs. We have worked all day long these days since we left Tsihombe, entering the items into our station books and the many other errands concerning our travel. We are living in the guest house and have our meals with Hofstads. We leave Fort Dauphin by plane day after tomorrow, so we do not have much time left. Seems so strange to think of it; it does not seem real.

June 12. This evening all the missionaries gathered at Hofstads for a little farewell. Leo Lellelid led the meeting with a short Bible Study and prayer. Dad responded with a short talk. Coffee and cakes were served. We have enjoyed the hospitality of the Hofstads.

On June 13 we left Fort Dauphin by plane. All the missionaries in Fort Dauphin, Arndt and family, and the Borges came out to the airfield to see us off. The Bible School sang a song. We had a strange feeling saying goodbye to everyone and everything in Fort Dauphin. The plane ride was smooth and uneventful. The food was excellent, but too much for us. The Dyruds are traveling with us to Paris. Between Cairo and Paris we went high above the heavy clouds. We were happy when we landed safely. Miss Nybroten had made arrangements for us and the Dyruds at Hotel Nice, a nice family hotel.

Today we had a shock; dad discovered that he could not find his American check book with only two blank checks left and three $100 checks from Midthun for our stay in Paris and train fare form New York to Minneapolis. We have been hunting through his pockets several times hoping we might find them. How can we sleep tonight with this on our minds? What can we do now? We took the bus way out to the airport the next day to see if there could be any possibility of getting in touch with someone who could investigate. But to no avail, though we did make a complaint. We hope no one can succeed in cashing the checks. This afternoon we went to Cooks and Company to get our tickets and there we discovered that no money had come from the treasurer in Fort Dauphin to pay for our tickets.

June 20. We were invited to missionary Jacobson for supper and he had taken care of our tickets out of his own pocket because the money had not yet arrived.

On June 21 we left Hotel Nice and moved to *"Centre d'Orientation,"* where Miss Nybroten is staying. We have a very nice room, 750 francs per day. The prices here are terrific. Three days at Hotel Nice cost us 11,710 francs.

June 25. This is our last day in Paris. We went down town this morning and walked down *Avenue de George V* to *Arc de Triomphe*. Yesterday we walked to *Trocadéro,* a popular tourist attraction created for the World's Fair in Paris. We are ready for tomorrow morning when we shall leave for our boat train for Le Havre. Today we arrived at *Gare Ste. Lazare* in good time. The train left at 8:30am and arrived at Le Havre 11am. We found our cabin but to our disappointment it was very tiny. The noon meal was good. We left Le Havre at 1:30pm. Now we have sailed three hours with a very fine ocean. The ship rides steadily but it vibrates.

June 30. It has been four days since we left Le Havre. Fine sailing, everyone is in good spirits and with a good appetite. Some are drinking and smoking. Dad has a book to read.

July 2. We are getting ready to land. We had a good look at the skyline of New York. It took us a long time to go ashore and our baggage was among the last to come on land. It took a long time before we got a customs officer to look at our luggage. When we were through, we looked to see if the Smiths (Tack's in-laws who live in New York) were in the waiting room. Then I heard our name and spelled out in letters. So we got a porter and went to the waiting room. And there they were. How wonderful it was to see them. They had a nice car and they got all our baggage in and off we went to New Paltz, about 80 miles away. On the way we stopped at Howard's Inn for dinner, a very fine place. The Smith's have a very nice home which they built themselves. It is out in the country with a heavy growth of trees and shrubs around the yard. A wren is singing outside the house so beautifully. What a lovely place for retirement.

July 5, 1956. Finally we are ready for the last leg of our long journey. We enjoyed our visit with the Smiths very much. They took us out for rides to visit the country side and saw so many beautiful homes. We boarded the train in Pughkeepsie at 5:40pm and had a roomette all to ourselves. We enjoyed the luxury of travel but were disappointed that our train was two hours late in arriving to Chicago, so we lost our connection. We took the next train at 11:30am and arrived in St. Paul at 6:15pm. We were surprised to see so many of our dear ones there to meet and greet us. Carl showed up first, then Tack and Mark, Agnes, Gloria, LaVonne, Betty, Augusta, Kittel, Craig, and Ricky. We were sorry they had to wait so long since we did not arrive on schedule. They had been in St. Paul at 2:30pm and waited a long time. It was thrilling to see them all and to realize that we had reached our destination safely. We are continually mindful of God's mercy and care for us. We went to the home of Kittel and Anna where they had a big dinner waiting for us. We stayed with them over night and the next day they took us to Northfield where Tack and Carl and their families were living for the time being. Tack and Betty and their two sons, Mark and Ricky, were packing to get ready to depart for the French Camerouns, to begin his work as a lay missionary. Carl and LaVonne and Craig were returning to Harvard Divinity School for his second year of working on his theological doctorate. We worked hard for weeks to get our house fixed up on Orchard Street in Northfield.

We started planning for our new house to be built on 712 Sumner Avenue. Tack and Carl bought a lot from the next door neighbor Campbell for $2,300 and hired Boyd to build the house for $15,000 to be ready for occupancy in April, 1957. We pray that God will bless this move.

POSTSCRIPT BY THE EDITOR

My mother continued to write in her diary after my parents retired in Northfield in 1957. After father died on October 2, 1975 in Northfield, Minnesota at the age of 87, mother lived alone in her house in Northfield until 1979 when she went to live with Agnes and Leonard in Thousand Oaks, California. This proved to be a blessed decision because there she could reunite not only with Agnes and Leonard and family but also with Arlene and Jim and family as well as with Tack and Betty and family. The last entries in her diary were written in March, 1985. Mother died February 5, 1988 in Thousand Oaks at the ripe old age of 94.

When I reflect on what I have learned from mother's diary, I feel I have come to know my parents better now than ever before. Her frequent entries reveal what they were thinking and experiencing at the time of writing. The four of us children, Agnes, Arlene, Tack and I, were not privy to their thoughts for most of our time in Madagascar because we were at the Missionary Children's Home in Fort Dauphin nine months of the year while they were miles away at their station of work. I have taken away eight impressions of mother's self-revealing personal record of the life and work of our parents on the mission field in Madagascar and of their round trip travels between America and Madagascar, which took them to many continents, countries, and islands and across many oceans, seas, and rivers.

First impression. The word "sacrifice" comes overwhelmingly to mind. Their decision to get married and to volunteer for the mission field virtually coincided, and from that day forward they would live a sacrificial life away from home, family and friends, not knowing whether or to what end their decision would take them. This was the second time for father to embark on a path that would lead him to an unknown country, first leaving Norway for America, and second leaving America for Madagascar, all in the span of a mere fifteen years. That could disorient any normal person with a bad case of vertigo. As for mother, Madagascar would plausibly be the last place on earth she would choose to live and work and raise a family. I never remember either father or mother say a word about how much they had sacrificed in the course of their missionary service. Rather, they often remarked that it was their privilege to serve God and the gospel in evangelizing the natives and planting the church in Madagascar.

Second impression. "Family" is a word that recurs throughout mother's diary. Mother and father loved their four children unconditionally and their hearts ached profoundly when they had to be absent from them, which of necessity happened more often than not. But their love for family extended widely to include their own fathers and mothers, brothers and sisters, uncles and aunts, and cousins distant and near, whether they happened to be in Norway or the United States. In the course of their travels back and forth to Madagascar they made three extended visits to Norway, to see all the living Braatens on my father's side and all the living Titruds on my mother's side. Mother was diligent in keeping in touch with them by correspondence. Often feeling lonely and isolated in their station of work, they longed to receive mail from abroad and were faithful in exchanging letters. They expressed great delight when they heard any good news of the accomplishments of their children. Family always meant so much to them.

Third impression. "Work" was the bread and butter of the life story of both father and mother. Father had to work on his dad's farm as soon as he was old enough to tend sheep and goats. He left the farm as a teen-ager to work in the little town of Bö. He learned the craft of a shoemaker and also worked as a clerk in a general store. When he came to the States at the age of nineteen, he worked on various farms at very low wages, and he kept working hard to pay his way through high school and Concordia College in Morehead, Minnesota and after that Luther Seminary in St. Paul. That work ethic continued throughout his life, even in his retirement years. He came to Madagascar before any of the missionaries owned cars. Dad rode a motorcycle. The motorcycle often broke down so he had to learn to be his own mechanic. The roads were so bad he had to deal with blown out tires. When he built churches, he worked like one of the regular carpenters hopping from one rafter to another.

Mother was the eldest of four children. When her mother died, Clara had to assume all the household chores, taking care of the three younger children, and as a result she was not able to attend school beyond the eighth grade. No high school and no college, and nothing but work until at the age of twenty eight she married Torstein. All of those years proved to be invaluable preparation for the hard life she and Torstein shared during their thirty five years of service as missionaries in Madagascar. The cards they were dealt from start to finish in life gave them no time, leisure, or money for sports, toys, or games. Boring? Not really! Necessity? For sure!

Fourth impression. "Sickness" was the most constant companion of life for both father and mother from their first year on the mission field until the last. It would probably be no exaggeration to say that neither one enjoyed a year of health without illness of one kind or other. They suffered from the usual tropical diseases, especially malaria. In their early days medical science had not yet developed vaccines to prevent or medicines to cure malaria. They also suffered from bouts of dysentery. It was not until their last term on the mission field that they had refrigeration. One can't tell bad food by looking at it, and food was not in abundance ever, so they had to think twice before throwing any of it away. Seldom did they have doctors to diagnose whatever illnesses they were suffering or to prescribe medicines to cure them. They had to rely on their own knowledge and resources.

Dad had many health issues, stomach problems, swollen legs, and epileptic seizures. Twice such seizures occurred while he was driving his car and both times he survived by the grace of God, otherwise called miracles. In hindsight it was a big mistake that mother never learned to drive a car. That would have spared them a lot of grief and worry. Mother had some undiagnosed illnesses that weakened her and kept her in bed for days. The best days of their life together from the standpoint of health were the years they were blessed to enjoy after retirement in Northfield.

Fifth impression. "Faith" was the firm foundation of the life of my father and mother from start to finish. Faith in the living God of the Bible was the solid rock of their existence expressed in words and deeds. They opened every morning with devotions after breakfast, reading from the Bible and spontaneous prayer led by father. The children heard these prayers whenever they were home, very long prayers that seemed to encompass everything going on in the world and the church. Sunday church attendance was a staple for the whole family and Sunday school for the children from first grade through high school. I don't recall any of us balking at these expected practices, experienced in the long run as both law and gospel. The faith of father and mother was nurtured on the ecclesial traditions of Norwegian Lutheran pietism which stemmed from the nineteenth century revivals of Hans Nielsen Hauge in Norway. This tradition was exported to the United States by the thousands of Norwegian immigrants in the late nineteenth century, many of whom settled in Minnesota and the Dakotas.

Sixth Impression. "Travel" is an essential part of missionary experience. It was already in evidence in the *Book of Acts* which tells about the three extensive missionary journeys that Paul and some of his companions made in the Mediterranean Basin. Mother's diary records not only how much they traveled going back and forth to Madagascar, but also how much they enjoyed sightseeing in numerous countries and cities in Africa, Europe, and Asia that most people only get to read about or see on maps of a World Atlas. On every journey they usually managed to take a circuitous route that took them to places they had never seen before. They did this not only for themselves but they wanted their children to experience the benefits of world travel. And we did. When we studied geography, our eyes would light up and we could exclaim, "I've been there; I've seen that and I remember when."

Seventh impression. News that accurately reported world events was in short supply for my father and mother whether they were on vacation in Lebanon or at their station of work. They were always hungry for up to date news; they read every church paper that came from the States, listened to the world news every evening on the radio, but they had to rely on the French press for information on what was happening on the island. My folks were in Madagascar during the Malagasy nationalist rebellion against French colonial rule that started in 1947, but the reports of what was happening were one-sided, as could be expected. The missionaries heard that the Malagasy revolutionaries planned to kill all the white people on the island, which of course included them. That was hard for them to believe, and in fact no such massacre took place anywhere on the island. The French military carried out a ruthless conter-offensive that included mass executions and torture, burning down villages, and capturing or killing the majority of the nationalist leaders. While hundreds of the French military lost their lives in the insurrection, the Malagasy casualties were estimated to be as high as 100,000. Some of the Malagasy pastors were accused of being complicit in the rebellion, were tortured and put in prison.

In his memoirs Uncle Kittel wrote about this difficult time for the mission. Should the mission remain neutral, support the French administration, or take the side of the Malagasy nationalists? The superintendent of the mission in Fort Dauphin chose to support the French government officials. Uncle Kittel made it clear that he did not agree, convinced that if the mission overtly took the side of the French against the Malagasy natives, that would deal a fatal blow against the mission. The missionaries may as well pack their bags and go home. Much to the credit of the interventions of uncle Kittel and aunt Anna in behalf of the Malagasy pastors and mission workers who were falsely accused and imprisoned, the mission survived the ordeal and was able to continue its evangelistic and educational work effectively.[5]

The reason that I mention this episode in the life of the Lutheran mission in south Madagascar is that most of the missionaries, including my parents, did not know much about what was going on at the time of the uprising. They lived out in the sticks away from the cities where the action was taking place, and they had no access to reliable news to inform them. They heard rumors, lots of them, mostly spread by the French officials, calculated to spread fear.

Eighth impression. Revival is a word that connotes an awakening of someone or some movement that has become dormant. I learned about revivals reading through the preaching of Jonathan Edwards and the revival of Christianity in Norway through the evangelistic ministry of Hans Nielsen Hauge in the nineteenth century, but we never expected anything of the sort to occur in Madagascar. The Malagasy heard and responded to the gospel preached by the missionaries for the first time. The Lutheran missionaries like my dad and uncle Kittel never talked about the need for a revival, since they found themselves in a raw evangelistic situation, preaching the gospel and teaching the catechism to those who have never heard it before. However, in the 1950s news about a revival sweeping across Madagascar began to spread. The Malagasy Lutheran Church experienced a religious revival due to the evangelistic activity of a lay woman prophetess, who was called Nenilava, which means "Tall Mother").[6] She was born in 1918 of non-Christian parents. Her father was a tribal chief, a famous healer and diviner. When she was ten years old, she began to see visions and hear voices. She married a Lutheran catechist who taught her Luther's *Small Catechism*, and baptized her. She

---

[5] Alice Bartholomay, daughter of uncle Kittel and aunt Anna, has made available their memoirs, written after they retired in Northfield, Minnesota, two blocks from my parents' home. The title of Anna's memoir is "All The Way He Leads" and the title of Kittel's memoir is "Reflections From the Past."

[6] An informative book has been published on the religious revival in Madagascar, co-authored by James B. Vigen and Sarah Hinlicky Wilson entitled, *Nenilava, Prophetess of Madagascar. Her Life and the Ongoing Revival She Inspired* (Pickwick Publications, Eugene, Oregon, 2021).

believed that Jesus was calling her to preach the gospel of repentance and forgiveness, to drive out demons from people possessed, and to heal through prayer and the laying on of hands. Nenilava's method was to train volunteer lay persons whom she called shepherds to accompany her on her travels throughout Madagascar.

The reaction of the missionaries was mixed. A few of the younger missionaries influenced by the charismatic movement among Lutherans in America were supportive of her work. Most of the missionaries went about their work as usual, which did not include driving out demons, performing miracles of healing, and speaking in tongues. The missionaries spoke many languages but not in tongues and they certainly practiced the arts of healing, inasmuch as many of them where nurses trained in America to use the modern methods based on medical science. The heathen witch doctors practiced exorcism and used various potions to perform miracles of healing. Such practices were experientially strange to the missionaries, even though their very own Bibles are full of stories about dreams and visions, prophecies and speaking in tongues, exorcisms and miracles, demons and evil spirits, sacrifices and offerings. The pre-Enlightenment Malagasy culture felt at home reading of such things in both the Old and New Testaments.

Photos

Torstein Folkvard and Clara Agnes Braaten

Torstein's parents, Folkvard and Aslaug Braaten

Clara's parents, Martin Titrud and Martha Ostmoe

Father and mother, with Agnes and Arlene

Father in his study reading as usual

Supper time for father and mother

See where the good looking Braatens come from

An Amilcar, Dad's first automobile, a sporty French convertible

Mother in the kitchen

Father and mother with Anna and Kittel Braaten, dad's older brother

Malagasy women deliver milk in bottles to the mission station.

A Malagasy beggar at the mission station

Main Street in Merimandroso, a suburb of Fort Dauphin

A typical scene of pounding out the rice kernels from the husks

A native dancer playing an accordion

The Malagasy Lutheran Church we attended

All dressed up in their finest for church

A baobab sacred majestic tree endemic to Madagascar

A church in Tranoroa that dad built, an outstation of Bekily

Another church that dad built, in Beraketa

A Mahogany wood carving of Jesus by a Malagasy artist

Ransfjord, the Norwegian freighter we took
from Madagascar to France

Our family on board the Ransfjord with
Laila Syvesind and Captain Thon

PART TWO

Tales of a Missionary Kid Growing Up in Madagascar

My parents, Torstein Folkvard and Clara Agnes Braaten, were blessed with four children, three of them born in Madagascar and one in the United States. I had two older sisters and one older brother. Agnes Theodora was born on Thanksgiving Day, October 31, 1923 in Fort Dauphin. Mother wrote in her diary about how giving birth to Agnes was extremely difficult and that it nearly cost her her life. Arlene Marie was born two years later on Christmas Day, December 25, 1925, also in Fort Dauphin. Folkvard Martin was also born two years later on Labor Day, September 5, 1927, in Fort Dauphin. I was also born two years later in St. Paul, Minnesota, on January 3, 1929, while my folks were on furlough from the mission field. We kids joked about the fact my three siblings, Agnes, Arlene, and Folkvard, were born on a holiday, whereas I missed being born on New Year's Day by only two days. I didn't feel so bad because having been born in the United States, I could brag that I was the only one eligible to become president.

I was born in my parent's home on Grantham Street in St. Paul, not in a hospital as might be expected. Our house was quarantined. No doctor was available because of the epidemic. Only the doctor and my dad were there to deliver the baby. They weighed me and claimed I was twelve pounds. Was the home scale really accurate? All my siblings were just over seven pounds.

After a year of furlough my parents returned to Madagascar to resume their work on the mission field. All four of us children lived with our parents in Bekily, all of us still too young to go to school at the Missionary Children's Home in Fort Dauphin. Agnes was the first to leave home for school, which meant she would be separated from her father and mother for many months at a time. Arlene was next to go, then Folkvard. Mother writes in her diary about how gut-wrenching those separations were, both for parents and children. I do remember when it first happened to me, how I sobbed gobs of tears and ran after their car as they drove away. Even when we got older, being separated from our parents for many months on end was a sobering and lonely experience. The fact that the four of us had each other for support helped to offset our sadness.

I remember only a little about my pre-school years in Bekily. I had trouble pronouncing my brother's name, Folkvard. I learned later that I was not the only one. I called him Fockwad. The Malagasy were worse at it. Folkvard sounded something like "Tukembaraky" to them. When he started school, it wasn't long before he acquired a new name, "Tack," or sometimes "Tuck." When Folkvard joined the army, the drill sergeant would make fun of his name, so Tack changed his name to Martin, his middle name. He was called Martin throughout his four years at St. Olaf College. From then on his official written name was "F. Martin Braaten." I often wondered, why would our parents ever think of naming my brother "Folkvard?" Folkvard was a common second name in the Braaten family. Our father's name is Torstein Folkvard, his three brothers were Hans Folkvard, Olaf Folkvard, and Kittlel Folkvard. Our cousin, Kittle's son, was named Arndt Folkvard. Obviously the consensus seemed to have been that Folkvard was just fine as a second name, but not as a first.

What else can I remember from those first six years at home before joining my siblings at school at the M. C. Home? Not much. I remember that my mother offered to pay me 5 centimes for every fly I would swat in the kitchen. I didn't make enough money to buy chewing gum. I remember going into the kitchen which was a small building detached from the house and got hold of a butcher knife. None of the servants saw me. I intended to use it to whittle a piece of wood to carve out a little boat. The knife slipped and made a huge gash in my ankle. I screamed to the top of my lungs and everybody came running. My mother was as good as any nurse and managed to stop the bleeding. But there was no doctor around to close the wound with stitches, so it left a big scar, still visible today. In the years before mother married dad, she was studying in Minneapolis to become a deaconess. She never received a degree to be a nurse, but on the mission field she had to provide health care for the Malagasy people who came to the station every morning with one kind of illness or another. Every morning she would appear on the veranda, meeting one patient at a time ready to provide whatever medical treatment was needed. They came with eye infections, swollen stomachs due to worms, body sores, dysentery, malaria, and syphilis. Medicines were available to treat such common illnesses.

I remember being cared for during the day by a Malagasy maid. Mother had lots of work to do and so did dad. Father and mother would often converse in Norwegian. The effect of this situation was that I had no one to talk to during the day. No kids around and no grown ups to sound out the English language. I was told later that it took me too long to shed baby talk. When I started first grade, my teachers noticed that I was somewhat behind the others. Yet, even in those earliest years I heard a lot of different languages. Besides English and Norwegian I heard people speaking Malagasy and French, and hardly understood a word they were speaking — just a cacophony of sounds. Whatever the downside to that, eventually it proved to be a blessing. In college I chose to major in English, which was my strongest major. In my freshman year I learned how to write a research paper, with all the proper *ibids* and *op.cit.s,* which paid dividends in my career as an author. I also majored in philosophy and French. Having grown up in a French colony, I had already learned how to speak some French.

As teenagers Tack and I had become best friends with some French boys and girls, to the consternation of some of the missionaries, for after all "they were Catholics." One time my dad called Tack and me into his office to have a talk with us. What about? He said he had received reports from missionaries in Fort Dauphin that we were spending time fraternizing with French boys and girls, and that they were Catholic. He asked if those reports were true? We both acknowledged that it was indeed the case. We asked something to the effect — I don't remember the exact words— "And, what's wrong with that? After all, we are not interested in their religion, nor they in ours." Dad did not respond in any negative way. Inwardly he probably was thinking, what else would one expect of two healthy teenage boys?

My French background unexpectedly came in handy later when I received a Fulbright Fellowship for a year of study at the University of Paris (Sorbonne). I proposed to focus on the philosophy of existentialism, to compare and contrast the thought of Jean-Paul Sartre (a French atheist) and Sören Kierkegaard (a Danish Lutheran). In the middle of the year I gave up the project because I had reached the conclusion that existentialist philosophy leads to a dead-end, no matter how you slice it. I was led to this conclusion in the course of reading the works of two French neo-Thomist philosphers, Étienne Gilson and Jacques Maritain.

At the age of six I joined Agnes, Arlene, and Folkvard at the home for missionary children (M. C. Home) in Fort Dauphin to attend school. The school was operated by the Foreign Mission Board of the Norwegian Lutheran Church in America, and included first grade through high school. Our teachers were qualified to teach all the subjects at the appropriate levels. The school building had two large rooms, one for children grades 1-6 and the other for junior and senior high, grades 7-12. Before World War II the missionaries usually attempted to have their 11th and 12th grade students transfer to America to finish high school. Once the war broke out, it became impossible to travel back home to America, so the juniors and seniors were stranded in Fort Dauphin to finish high school. This war time necessity affected the students involved in a negative way; when they eventually returned to the States, they felt like ugly ducklings, misfits, out of touch with what teenagers thought and how they acted.

I experienced some of the social awkwardness that such seniors felt when they returned to America. After I finished my junior year of high school in Fort Dauphin, I came to Minneapolis and lived with Kittel and Anna Braaten, my uncle and aunt. Immediately I applied for work and got a job as a bus boy at Bridgeman's Ice Cream Shop on Hennepin Avenue down town. The very first day of work I experienced that everything was new to me. When it was time for a break, the other bus boys and girls were given half an hour for lunch. They invited me to join them; I would have had no idea where to go. So we went to a nearby White Castle, a hamburger shop. All five of us sat up to the counter on stools. When the waitress came along to take our order, the guy next to me ordered a Malt and French Fries. I didn't know what that meant, but I was quick on the draw to avoid embarrassment, so I simply said, "Same thing." But that was a close call. I also remember bussing the huge soda glasses behind the counter; the customers would look at me and comment on how tan I was. They would ask, "Wow, where did you get that tan?" Here I was with a tan, so conspicuous in the middle of January in Minneapolis. So I lied by responding that I had been in Florida on vacation with my family. Another dodge from social embarrassment. There were other similar incidents having to do with dating.

In Madagascar no dating was going on. So obviously we missionary kids had to try to make up for lost time. I had my first date for the senior prom when I graduated from high school at Augustana Academy. At most high school proms seniors dress up, dine out, and dance the night away. At our prom we did dress up and dined out and then listened to a speech. Dancing was taboo. One professor of religion called dancing "vertical prostitution." Another wrote a pamphlet entitled, "Don't Play With Fire!" Dancing got a bad reputation among midwest Lutheran legalistic pietists. Of course, not only among Lutherans. Methodists too and others as well. But their teenagers were not stupid. They learned that they didn't have to dance to have a good time on a date. The back seat of a car could serve as a pretty good substitute.

At the M. C. Home we, the captive boarders, may have experienced loneliness apart from our parents, but we were never alone. There were always two or three others in the same grade. In my grade I had Paul Norlie and Fred Hallanger. Tack had his cousin Olaf and Erling Stolee. We were served three meals a day, breakfast, dinner, and supper. Every meal was opened and closed with a brief table prayer. The dining room had three tables, each seating eight persons, one for the youngest children, another for the older and the third for those in-between. Sunday evenings were a time for devotions, with Scripture and prayers. Every student was expected to recite a Bible verse, usually one learned in the morning of the same day in Sunday School. A favorite verse to recite, if a student couldn't remember any, was the shortest verse in the Bible, "Jesus wept." (John 11: 35). The food was prepared by a Malagasy cook and served by his assistant. The fare was always good and plentiful. We had to learn and observe good table manners, and anyone who acted out of line would be shunned or criticized by the others. Eating three meals a day with the same persons year after year made for life-long friendships.

Miss Celia Thompson was the matron for most of the years I was at the M. C. Home. In hindsight she should have had at least one assistant to help her oversee all the work she had in caring for over thirty students, supervise the cooks and houseboys, call the doctors and nurses when anyone was sick, make sure the rules were observed by every child and mete out the punishments to those of us who broke them. What a responsibility! If Protestants had saints, she would have deserved to be one of them for sure. She kept her cool in times of trouble, reliable and resourceful as a multi-tasker. Mother got a taste of what Celia Thompson endured for decades at the M. C. Home. In her last year on the mission field she was asked to fill in as the matron because Sister Anna Gjerness had to leave for America and there was no one else available. After serving for a few months Mother commented in her diary on how much she admired Miss Thompson for her many valiant years of service as our matron.

Those of us who experienced life at the M. C. Home never forgot the friendships we made that lasted our whole lives. In 1994 Agnes and I planned a Missionary Children's reunion that took place at St. Olaf College. Over sixty of us attended, most retired and some superannuated. The program we planned included joyous singing of the Malagasy hymns we had learned by attending church every Sunday in Fort Dauphin. Agnes, the most accomplished musician from the M. C. Home, accompanied all the hymn singing, playing the piano by heart. Arndt Braaten, our cousin, preached the sermon. That brought back memories of the hundreds of long-winded sermons we children had to listen to, preached in the Malagasy language. We could see the preachers' gestures and admire their sincerity and enthusiasm, as they pounded the pulpit, understanding but few of the words, words like "Zanahary" (God) and what a relief when they said "Amen!" Some of the missionaries had difficulty preaching in the Malagasy language and often made a *faux pas* that made the natives laugh. Here is one example told to me. A new missionary, I won't mention his name, preached his first sermon in the Malagasy language. He intended to assure the congregation, "There is a lot of room for every one in heaven." What he actually said was, "There are lots of oxen in heaven." "*Betsika ny omby any andanitra.*"[7] The Malagasy would love to hear that; they love their oxen. "Omby" means "oxen" and it sounds like the word for "room" to a foreigner.

It would take a book to write about all the shenanigans going on at the M. C. Home. My brother, Folkvard, and I shared the same room on the first floor of the Home. It was called *Trano Vato*, a large stone building. The windows had chicken wire for screens, not to keep the mosquitoes out but to keep us in. It didn't work. During the day we loosened the screws that held them fast and replaced them in holes made larger, so that we could easily escape through the windows at night. The rule was "lights out at 8pm." When we became teenagers, that seemed too early for us to hit the sack. Miss Thompson would enter our rooms to see if we were in bed. We used pillows to make it appear that we were under the covers, as she would hold a lit match in front of her. Our disguise worked to a tee. For us the rule was too restrictive. We would climb through the

---

[7] I am not sure of my Malagasy spelling. It's been 77 years ago.

window and escape for a time to spend with our French friends. Truth to tell, we didn't do anything bad; we only wanted some freedom.

The large stone building had no running water, which meant no indoor plumbing. We had to go outside to a faucet to fetch water in a pitcher to wash our face and brush our teeth. We had to use a *pot de chambre* at night to go potty and in the morning we had to empty it in the back yard, an unsanitary thing to do.

After supper and before bedtime students would gather in the living room, read magazines like *Life* and *Time,* play dominoes, or simply chat with each other. Some would try to fraternize with the opposite sex as much as they dared. I'll say it again, dating was taboo. Kissing, even for older teenagers, was done only in dreams. The girls were especially carefully watched, never allowed to leave the fenced in campus for any reason except with adult chaperones, usually our teachers. There was no such restriction for the boys, some thing the girls resented. Boys could take their bikes and ride away wherever they wanted. There wasn't much to see, so we would just ride downtown and look at the ships in the harbor.

During the warm season all of us would be accompanied by an adult to an hour of swimming at one of the beaches well protected by reefs. That means it was completely safe from sharks. There was a cabin for changing into our swimming suits, one room for the girls and one for the boys. Boys will be boys! The wall between the two cabins was made of pine boards. Pine boards have knots. When a knot is removed, one can see into the other room, just right for peeping toms. This is a true story. One peeping tom looked through a knot and saw an eye from the other room returning the favor. The girls knew what was going on, and learned how to dress or undress without baring any skin.

While we are on the subject of voyeurism, one of the boys, a close friend of mine, told us about a risky encounter he had. Lebanon was a peninsula where the missionaries had their vacation cottages, a little over one kilometer from Fort Dauphin. One day an unmarried French couple, their names were Monsieu Teramosi and Madame De Coq, took a beautiful scenic walk from Fort Dauphin to Lebanon and disappeared behind some bushes. My friend, a year younger than I, followed them and approached the bushes where he supposed they were. He came close, peered through the bushes and saw them copulating. The man heard the rustling of the leaves, pulled on his pants, took after my friend and caught him by the neck. The man chastised him and let him go, no doubt realizing he could be in great trouble if he did any harm to this missionary kid. After all, he knew he was not supposed to be doing this with another man's wife. That was a no-no even for the French colonialists.

At the Home there were bigger boys and little kids and those in-between. Most of the time we all got along very well, but not always. I recall an incident when a bigger boy, two years older than I, was picking on me, intimidating me, and I had enough of it. We were both on the porch when he was bullying me. I lost my temper, went after him with my fists flailing, and took him down. He quit and never bothered me again. I felt bad about it because I learned he had been weakened by a bout of malarial fever. I remember another time when I felt I was being threatened by two boys around my same age. I don't remember what the scuffle was all about, only that the two of them thought that I would have to back down. I didn't. I charged after them, punching first one and then the other, until they went away crying. I was not proud of that, but it taught me not to tolerate bullying of any kind.

Speaking of bullying, it has become a real problem in grade schools today. When I was nine years old and my brother Tack was ten, we lived in St. Anthony Park, St. Paul, when my parents were on furlough, residing at Mission Cottage No. 7 on the hill just above Luther Seminary. We were outside a lot, playing around with the neighborhood kids. One day a bigger boy started picking on Skippy Johnson, a friend of ours who lived a block away. He was younger and smaller than the two of us, and couldn't defend himself. We couldn't stand by and watch him being bullied. So we decided to take him on, not knowing what the outcome would be. Tack, who was good at tackle football and played on the Cub Scouts Team, dove for his legs and upended him. The two of us, Skippy and I, started punching him, twisting our fingers in his temple until he started to bawl. We had him down on the ground and he gave up. He never bothered us again. The moral of the story is, bullies don't belong on the playground. The truth is, I never liked to fight, never enjoyed physical altercations. I am nearly a 100% a pacifist.

I did not enjoy grade school very much. All I remember from the first grade is learning how to read words from a big chart. The words were, "Come. Come and play. Come and play with me today." Those few words were chosen perhaps because they contain more than half of the twenty six letters of the alphabet. The next lines continued in the same vein, until we became familiar with all the letters of the alphabet and how to sound them out. Our teacher was Clara Dysland, a tough no-nonsense task master. She wouldn't tolerate any mischief; any act of disobedience was answered with a spanking. In those days teachers got away with spanking and our parents did not protest. Sometimes she would make us go to the blackboard and write this line twenty times; "Obedience is the first thing to learn at school." We also learned to write, using the Palmer Method. Thank you, Clara Dysland, you taught us how to read and write. But that is not all. You taught us the basics of mathematics, how to add, subtract, multiply, and divide — really fast. She had us go to the blackboard, write a long column of numbers, and made us race to see who finished first. I don't know how to account for it, but I was the fastest kid at the blackboard, including competing against upper-class members. The ability with numbers has stayed with me to this day, and it comes in handy every year when I have to do my taxes. I never have to use an adding machine to help me with the numbers. Other than these few recollections, I remember the long tedious hours of being bored in school. I longed to hear the bell ring at the end of the school day so we could do what we enjoyed the most, play soccer or soft ball or ride our bikes around town.

My three years of High School were more interesting and challenging for me. I learned to study and cram for exams. We learned techniques at memorization. I memorized many Psalms and chapters of the Bible. I wanted to get good grades. We had to show our report cards to our parents and they had to sign that they had seen them. Dad wanted to see nothing less than a perfect record. Our most challenging subjects were World History, Algebra, English, Science, Latin, and Bible. Science was our weakest subject, no doubt because none of our teachers had any interest or knowledge in any of the sciences. And our school had no science laboratory for experiments. When school was in session, total silence prevailed. Conduct was graded, and any whispering whatsoever resulted in conduct marks. So guess what, conduct was usually my lowest grade. The school had no indoor plumbing so students had to ask for permission to go to the outhouse, raising one or two fingers, depending on which urge was calling for attention. The desks were close to each other, so a little flirting with someone of the opposite sex was, well, both easy and innocent.

The guys got to wear their first long pants the day they were confirmed and they also wore new leather shoes. Most of the time we went barefoot or wore handmaid sandals made out of automobile tires. Uncle Kittel was my confirmation instructor. To the six of us in our class he seemed to be a very strict and humorless instructor. The beneficial result was that we studied hard to learn and to memorize the whole of Luther's *Small Catechism*, including every word that explains, "What is meant by this?" When I became a pastor twelve years later I discovered that many of my fellow pastors in the Twin Cities thought that was punishment too cruel for the confirmands. They preferred hay rides and thinking more positive thoughts. And today our churches are reaping the consequences of such laxity.

I have never forgotten one exchange I had with uncle Kittel. He was explaining the way of salvation, using the three *solas* of our Lutheran tradition, by grace alone, through faith alone, on account of Christ alone. If salvation is only by faith, only by believing in Christ, will all those who die without such faith be forever damned to hell? The obvious answer is "yes." But I thought to ask, though I was no budding theologian, what about all the Malagasy people who have never had a chance to hear the gospel? What about the many whom the missionaries have not been able to reach? Only a small percentage of the Malagasy people had become Christian, but how about the majority who have not, through no fault of their own? How does that square with an all-powerful, all-knowing and all-loving heavenly Father? Uncle Kittel had obviously thought about this matter before, because he was ready with an answer. He referred to Peter 3: 19, which is the source of the speculation that many church fathers held that on Holy Saturday, between Good Friday and Easter Sunday, Christ went to preach to the "spirits in prison." Who are they? They are, first of all, the patriarchs and prophets of the Hebrew Scriptures, as well as all who died out of earshot of hearing the gospel. That includes most of the people who ever lived from the beginning of time until now. That is admittedly pure speculation, still one that has prompted a lot of thought. The topic is one that I have written about in a number of books and articles, including my most recent book, *Saved by Grace through Faith* (ALPB, 2022).

The day before I was confirmed, my mother said she wanted to talk to me. It was a heart to heart conversation. She wanted to know whether I realized the gravity of the ceremony, that it was not merely a perfunctory one like many others, but one that called for a decision with lasting meaning for life. Do I really want to affirm that I was a believer in Christ and a member of his church, no strings attached? I answered yes, to her satisfaction, and I believe she was happy about that the rest of her life. Not that I have always had smooth sailing without plenty of doubts and questioning along the way. Our Lord Jesus loved doubting Thomas as much as the other disciples. It was he who exclaimed to the risen Jesus, "My Lord and my God!" (John 20: 28)

Every year our school put on a Christmas program at the M. C. Home for the missionaries, including our parents if they came in time from their mission station to begin their vacation on Lebanon. Most of the time my parents were among those who were not able to make it that early. They felt they had to be present for the Christmas celebrations in their own congregation in Bekily or Behara or wherever they happened to be stationed. Our Christmas program included songs and recitations by the students, and every student had some part to perform, whether musical or a piece to deliver. I remember the unpleasant feeling of being scared to death of standing up in front of everybody, fearing that I might forget my piece. One of the teachers would have in her hand the piece each one was to recite and be ready to coach when someone needed some help. It was not fun. But sometimes it was funny when some poor guy would be reciting his piece and some of his buddies would make faces at him to make him laugh or forget his part.

At the M. C. Home every student had to take piano lessons. As students we would have benefited enormously if the Mission had provided instruments needed for a band, like violins, cellos, trumpets, saxophones, drums, etc. How thoughtless to suppose that every student should try to learn the same musical instrument. Only a few of the students learned to play the piano with great skill, and my sister Agnes was one of them. Gerhard Cartford was another. My dad owned a guitar and knew how to play, but when he became hard of hearing, he lost both his interest and ability. Mother learned enough to enjoy strumming on the old guitar and even tried to teach me a few tunes. Arlene learned how to play the hymns of the church, so she could play for her own enjoyment or for Sunday school. Tack and I took piano lessons like all the rest, but neither of us was blessed with a high musical I.Q. We passed on these musically deficient genes to our children, none of whom have excelled in playing the piano or any other musical instrument. My daughter Maria is an exception; she inherited from her mother, LaVonne, an ability to sing in choirs and to sing solos at weddings and other occasions. LaVonne graduated from St. Olaf College with a music major, sang in the chapel choir and played the trombone in the band at Waldorf College and St.Olaf College. She also sang in prestigious choirs in the years we were in Paris and Heidelberg. So except for Maria's vocal talent, the rest of us simply enjoy singing in church and at family reunions, but do not possess the talent to perform for others.

The children at the M. C. Home suffered more than their share of various illnesses. Malaria, typhoid, and yellow fever were the most common. During the time that I was there, only one person died of illness. Hortense Quanbeck died of yellow fever. A French doctor was available on call to diagnose and treat whatever ailed us at the Home, and missionary nurses were skilled in taking care of us. Every evening Miss Thompson would be available to care for anyone with a problem.

The most common was known as flees making a home in the toes of our dirty unwashed feet. They were called "*parasy*." She or or one of the bigger kids would tackle them with a sewing needle, picking around each one until it was ready to be dug out. Or, with practice we could do it for ourselves. Of course, we all took our turns at getting the common cold. Agnes, Arlene, Tack, and I were never so seriously sick that our parents had to be notified or summoned to come and attend to us, as was the case with others from time to time. We did not know much about the key to good health. We took things for granted. There was no one to remind us to brush our teeth mornings and evenings. We had no tooth paste, only soap and salt. We heard that the Malagasy girls at the Mission school in Manafiafy used dried chicken dirt to brush their teeth.

When we became teenagers, we had plenty of ways to expend our energy. Bikes were important to us, our main means of transportation. The problem was that there were no new tires available to purchase. We patched them until we couldn't pump them up anymore. My parents bought two American bikes for Tack and me at Montgomery Ward in San Francisco before we left for Madagascar in 1939. They meant well, but American bikes were not made for the kind of rough terrain we had in Madagascar, compared to the French bikes. Our bikes had balloon tires instead of narrow ones, and they had no gears, which made for slow and hard pedaling. I was always at the tail end when a group of us would venture on a long trip out of town.

Next to biking boating was important to us. Tack already showed at that time that he had the innate ability to make things with tools, akin to his father's. Making and sailing boats became our favorite pastime when we became teenagers. We started by making toy sailboats and competed to see whose was fastest. Then we made outrigger canoes for sailing. We made the boats out of iron corrugated roofing. We laid them on the concrete tennis court and flattened them out with the front wheel of a wheelbarrow loaded with rocks. Then we wrapped the iron sheets around ribs made with wood. We added a keel and a rudder, and we thought they were fit for sailing. One day we carried them down to the shore in Fort Dauphin. It was a beautiful day with an offshore wind. We had two boats; Erling and Leif Stolee in one, Tack and I and Roald Carlson in the other. And away we went, intending to sail our boats around a freighter anchored in the harbor far from shore. Soon we discovered that the two boats would do fine heading straight out into the ocean, but would not respond to tacking. When we tried to tack them against the wind, the boats capsized and filled up with water. Fortunately, a tug boat noticed our predicament and came to rescue the five of us, but our boats sunk and were lost forever. We learned a lesson; do not head out to sea unless you have a sea-worthy boat. A few of the missionaries were downtown looking down from the hill and observed our plight. We knew we were in trouble. We were campus bound for weeks and prohibited from sailing. As the saying goes, "You can't keep a good man down." A few months elapsed and Tack was getting restless. He wanted to build a seaworthy craft, and that's exactly what we did. Tack was in charge of building a beautiful sail boat that could take us wherever we wanted to go.

Next to bikes and boats, we also wanted to excel in sports. But we had few opportunities. We had a good tennis court next to the M. C. Home, but when World War II started, we had no way to string our rackets or to buy new tennis balls. We also had a basketball and a small court to learn to shoot baskets and dribble the ball. But the war ended that too, since the ball wore out and couldn't be replaced. That left us with volley ball and soccer. Fortunately for us, the military in town organized volleyball and soccer teams, and wanted some opposition. Five of us from the Home and several of our French friends, Gilbert Cabiro and Raymond Faget, formed the nucleus of a team, with the addition of some town folks. We were ready to play and we thought we got pretty good at it. When I came to the States, I found out that we really were not very good at either sport. We had no coaches, with no one to teach us the finer points about how to play either sport.

In Madagascar every one lives close to the earth, and we were no exceptions. Animal life is a major part of it. We learned to raise chickens, rabbits, turtles, geese, turkeys, pigs, goats, sheep, and birds. My favorite was raising chickens. My cousin Olaf was also devoted to raising chickens. He ordered special breed eggs from Tananarive, like Rhode

Island Reds and Leghorns, hoping that they would be better at laying eggs. It didn't happen; the tropical climate was more suitable to hybrid species. I remember being asked to kill a chicken and pluck the feathers to ready it for cooking. I took an axe and chopped off the head and let it run around flapping its wings. I learned the meaning of the expression, "He was running around like a chicken with its head cut off." I didn't try that again.

There was one truly negative thing about growing up as a missionary kid in Madagascar. We had no money. We were not given any allowance and there was no way to earn a centime. We were broke all the time. If we needed something, like material for building our boats — boards, sandpaper, nails, screws, putty and paint — we helped ourselves to it from any source within our reach. Then something unexpected happened. A Norwegian freighter was torpedoed in the Indian Ocean. The sailors escaped on lifeboats and abandoned them on the beach south of Manafiafy, around fifty kilometers from Fort Dauphin. They walked to Fort Dauphin and checked in at the Mission station. Uncle Kittle and Aunt Anna were able to greet them, fed them, provided them a place to sleep, and gave them whatever medical care they needed. We heard about their two lifeboats abandoned on the beach. We jumped on our bikes and rode out to find them. One was too far from shore, we could do nothing with it. The other was partly buried in the sand on the beach. We worked for hours to bail out the water and shovel out the sand, hoping to salvage the boat; eventually we realized that was a losing proposition. A big wave would come and fill it up again. But we salvaged all we could from the lifeboat, chiefly the copper tanks. We knew they must be worth something. So we sold them to Cabi's dad who was the CEO of the Company Marseillaise. And finally we had some money in our pockets.

One would think that living on the sea coast, we would all learn how to fish. There were all kinds of fish that the natives would catch and bring to the mission station to sell. I suppose we thought that was something only the Malagasy did. Besides we had no fishing gear and no one to teach us anything about fishing. None of the missionaries cared about the sport of fishing. Fishing is something people did for food, not for sport. But Cabi taught us the dangerous sport of fishing with dynamite sticks. We would light a stick of dynamite and drop it into the water. In a few seconds it would explode and stun every living thing in close range. We would jump into the water, nab the groggy fish and toss them into the boat, scores of them. We only did this several times before we realized it was not a good sport. We had no use for the fish. It was plainly a stupid thing to do.

We loved to body surf in the big ocean waves. One day we were down by the ocean and some native boys speaking French told us not to do any surfing at a nearby beach. They said, "Watch out." They used the word *"requin."* We did not know the meaning of the word. We thought they were warning us about a hurricane. We thought to ourselves, that will make the waves bigger, much to our liking. Anyway, if a hurricane does come, we can leave the water right away. So we waded out; the waves were wonderful; we were having a great time. Suddenly someone yelled "shark." Then we saw a fin only a few yards from us. So we caught the next wave that swept us up onto the beach, safe and sound. Close call. An unforgettable experience.

Hunting crocodiles was something we knew nothing about, but our French friend Cabi did. He owned the gun and the bullets needed to shoot crocodiles. Cabi invited a few of us to join him on a hunting expedition. We drove out into the country and hired a native who knew the area. He led us to a nearby river where there were crocodiles. We saw one sunning itself on a nearby bank. Cabi and his guide approached as close as they dared without making a sound. Cabi's gun was loaded, he took aim, pulled the trigger, and bang, the Croc was hit and hurled itself into the water. Now it was in the water wounded, to be sure. Our native guide knew what to do. He saw the crocodile swishing around in the water, so he waded in and grabbed it in such away that it could not bite back. He brought it to shore, to our amazement.

After that experience I knew that hunting would never be a sport that I could enjoy. Killing for the fun of it did not seem like a lot of fun to me. This was confirmed when Tack and I were invited by a French friend, Jean de Heaulmes, who lived with his parents on a ranch near Berenty, a town not far from Bekily where our parents were stationed. We rode our bikes to his ranch and he took us out into the woods where there were plenty of birds. He had a gun and showed us how he could shoot one beautiful bird after the other. Not for me. Never again. It turned my stomach. I never even wanted to shoot a BB gun. "Thou shalt not kill."

Tack and I learned to drive our dad's car, a five passenger Renault sedan. I had my first accident the year I learned to drive. There were no speed limits or road signs. I was driving from Fort Dauphin to Lebanon with several friends in the back seat. Boy, was I proud. Then I saw a car coming toward us, so I swerved to avoid getting hit. I drove into the left lane and hit a lamp post. Louise Hofstad was in the back seat and the jolt caused her to chip her front tooth. I felt so bad. Dad was not hard on me because he had plenty of accidents himself. We got the front radiator fixed from leaking and a car shop straightened out the front grill.

Tack graduated from high school in 1946. When World War II came to an end, it was safe to travel again on ocean freighters. We learned that a boat was leaving from Tamatave, a seaport in the northern part of the island. Father and mother made haste to book passage for us. We traveled by bus to Tamatave, and when we arrived we learned that the captain of the ship wanted Tack to serve as a wiper in the engine room. He would not have to pay for his passage and would instead be paid a handsome daily wage, more money than he had ever seen in his life. Our trip back home was uneventful, but I remember how happy I was to leave Madagascar behind for the land of my birth.

In 1974 I returned to Madagascar with LaVonne on a sabbatical year of travel during which I was invited to give lectures at many seminaries around the world founded by missionaries. During that year I visited and lectured at seminaries in Japan, Hong Kong, Singapore, India, both in Madras and Bangalore, and Africa, both in Tanzania and Kenya. Finally we went to Madagascar to revisit all the old watering holes of my youth. The children at the M. C. Home had it very different from the time we were there. They could see their parents often. The cars and the roads were better, gas was plentiful, and the missionary salaries were equal to what pastors in the States were making. We stayed with Cabi and his wife; they were gracious hosts. But Cabi was the same. He abused his servants and did not treat them with the respect they deserved. Cabi drove us out to Behara where my folks had spent some years at the mission station. He took us to a village and told the chief that we were visitors from America, and that we want to buy silver bracelets. He let out the word and the natives came running out of their huts with an assortment of real silver bracelets. We bought a number of them to use as gifts, and I bought a unique one for a hundred dollars, unlike any I had ever seen. I have worn it since every day of my life, to remind me of my roots on the mission field in south Madagascar. Cabi leant us his car to drive to Tulear where we were to catch a plane to fly us to Paris. His chauffeur had been drinking all night, so when I saw that he was falling asleep at the wheel, I told him to switch places with me. So I drove the rest of the way. We returned to Chicago after months of travel, tired but happy to be back home and to reunite with our four children who were cared for by a responsible student couple at LSTC while we were gone.

This return visit to Madagascar gave me the occasion to reflect on what growing up there has meant to me in the long run. There were times when I resented spending my youth far away from the land of my birth. One word for me expressed that woeful sentiment, "elsewhere." When I experienced boredom and realized that I was missing out on what teenagers in the United States took for granted, I wanted to be "elsewhere." Eventually I overcame that feeling and became grateful for all the special benefits we enjoyed as missionary kids. One obvious benefit was that we acquired a global perspective without any effort on our part. All the travel back and forth between Madagascar and the United States took us to many places and corners of the world that we otherwise would see only on a map. Off the top of my head I can cite quite a few: Norway, France, England, Belgium, Netherlands, Thailand, Japan, South Africa, Singapore, Reunion, Mauritius, Saigon, Zanzibar, and Philippines. Our travels sparked a keen interest in stamp collecting. We clipped all the stamps we received from abroad from the letters relatives and friends sent to our parents and teachers. We traded stamps with others whose hobby was stamp collecting. There was hardly a place on earth that we did not come to know from this hobby. I kept it going for quite a while and then passed on this interest to my eldest child, Craig.

Once Rev. Rolf Syrdahl, the executive director of the Foreign Mission Board of the Norwegian Lutheran Church in America, invited me to speak with him in his office. I was a pastor in North Minneapolis at that time, and he knew that would not be the last stop for me. He knew I had an earned doctorate in theology from Harvard University and that I was prepared to teach Christian theology. He asked if I would consider a teaching position at a theological school in Yaoundé, Cameroun. My brother, Folkvard Martin, a few years later became a missionary as a lay educator to Cameroun. My answer to Rolf Syrdal was that although I was a firm believer in the apostolic cause of world missions, I did not sense that God was calling me to be a missionary to Africa. Instead of that I expressed my commitment to world missions in two ways, first, by writing books and articles on missiology,[8] and second by visiting and lecturing at schools and seminaries founded by missionaries in Asia, Africa, and South America. I discovered to my surprise that some of my books had been translated into a number of foreign languages without my knowing it — French, Spanish, German, Portuguese, Latvian, Hungarian, and Korean.

I was always proud that so many in the Braaten tribe chose to express their ordination vows as missionaries abroad rather than remain home as pastors in the United States. There were a good number of them. The first generation included the three brothers from Norway, Olaf Folkvard in China, Kittel Folkvard and Torstein Folkvard in Madagascar, and the second generation included Arndt Folkvard Braaten and Agnes

---

[8] My first book on missiology was written when I was a visiting lecturer at the Lutheran Seminary in Japan, *The Flaming Center, A Theology of the Christian Mission* (Fortress Press, 1977). After that I wrote *The Apostolic Imperative, Nature and Aim of the Church's Mission and Ministry* (Augsburg Publishing House, 1985), followed by *No Other Gospel, Christianity Among World Religions* (Fortress Press, 1992) and *That All May Believe, A Theology of the Gospel and the Mission of the Church* (Eerdmans, 2008).

Theordora Akland in Madagascar, and Folkvard Martin Braaten in Cameroon, Africa. As I reflect on my fifteen years growing up on the mission field in Madagascar, I am grateful for what I learned there that prepared me to be a pastor and a theologian and even for the rather strict discipline that in hindsight I now regard was the necessary condition of the sound education we experienced at the M. C. Home in Fort Dauphin, Madagascar.

I close this chapter of reminiscences with a heart full of gratitude for all that God has accomplished in Madagascar through the ministry of my parents and all their fellow missionaries in Madagascar.

Photos

The four of us kids with two Malagasy boys to help push our wagon
Notice Agnes holding a monkey.

Agnes and Arlene with an ox cart hauling water

Missionary children, with two unkempt boys,
Tack and Carl, in the front row

The boat that Tack built sailing in the Fort Dauphin harbor

Natives caught crocodile hides to sell to make shoes and purses.

Cabi, our French friend

Cabi with the crocodile he shot

Tack with the crocodile he shot

ABOUT THE BOOK

Clara Agnes Braaten kept a diary from the year she married the author's father, Torstein Folkvard Braaten, in 1922 until she was ninety-four-years old.

Three weeks after they were married, they departed Minneapolis by train for New York City to board the Stavangerfjord, a fine Norwegian ocean liner, to cross the Atlantic Ocean on their way to Bergen, Norway.

The author's father had accepted a call from the Foreign Mission Board of the Norwegian Lutheran Church in America to become a missionary to Madagascar. The couple decided to visit Norway on their way to Paris, France, where they were to spend one year learning the French language.

In this book, the author draws on his mother's diaries to highlight why his parents obeyed the Great Commission and how they lived it every day in Madagascar. The book includes excerpts selected from his mother's diary as well as a brief narrative of what the author remembers about growing up in Madagascar.

Whether you're interested in missionary life, the Lutheran Church, the history of Madagascar, or genealogy, you'll enjoy *Living the Great Commission in Madagascar*.

ABOUT THE AUTHOR

Carl E. Braaten is professor emeritus of systematic theology at the Lutheran School of Theology at Chicago, where he taught from 1961 to 1991. He is an ordained minister of the Evangelical Lutheran Church in America and served as pastor of the Lutheran Church of the Messiah in Minneapolis, from 1958 to 1961. He is the author and editor of more than fifty books on various theological topics.

He was the founding editor of *Dialog: A Journal of Theology*. In 1992, he co-founded the Center for Catholic and Evangelical Theology and became its executive director. He is also the founder of the ecumenical journal, *Pro Ecclesia*, and its senior editor. He's retired and lives in Sun City West, Arizona.

Printed by BoD™in Norderstedt, Germany